How to Buy

Costa Rica Real Estate Without Losing Your Camisa

by Scott Oliver

Important Note:

This book contains the author's opinions. Some material in this book may be affected by changes in the law (or changes in interpretations of the law) or changes in market conditions since the manuscript was prepared. Therefore, the accuracy and completeness of the information contained in this book and the opinions based on it cannot be guaranteed.

Neither the author nor the publisher is engaged in rendering legal, tax accounting, or other similar professional services. If these services are required, the reader should obtain them from a competent professional. **The publisher and author specifically disclaim any liabilities** for loss incurred as a consequence of following any advice or applying information presented in this book.

This book was printed in Costa Rica.

To order additional copies of this book, please contact Scott Oliver of **www.WeLoveCostaRica.com** at **admin@WeLoveCostaRica.com** or telephone the author in Costa Rica - (506) 396-3924

PREFACE

A Personal Note From The Author

Buenos dias, querido amigo.

New York City is not for everyone and neither is Costa Rica.

Over the last 45 years, I have been fortunate enough to have lived in ten different countries, visited 13 others and now consider Costa Rica 'home'. However, after visiting, you may feel differently.

Some people advised me not to discuss any *negatives* but I feel that **you need to know** what this beautiful country is all about - the bad as well as the good because even when you love someone, you also accept that they are not quite *perfect*, right?

I am naturally enthusiastic about Costa Rica but do not want to mislead you in any way; my goal with this book and **www.WeLoveCostaRica.com** is to help you enjoy this *rich coast* – a place of stunning scenery, sunshine and smiles.

My home has never been burgled and the only unpleasant personal experiences I've had have been with foreigners here and not Costa Ricans.

I do not claim to be an *expert* in everything Costa Rican but, **I will promise you** that if you give me an opportunity to help you find your new home in Costa Rica, **I will do my best** to find the right experts for you.

Even if the only research you do into Costa Rica real estate is to read this little book, **you will be more informed** than the majority of people who call themselves 'brokers' here.

Best wishes from your *amigo* in Costa Rica.

Scott Oliver, San José, 2005

I dedicate this book to **two truly remarkable young people**

Ian and Catherine.

ACCLAIM FOR THE AUTHOR

With his new book, *How To Buy Costa Rica Real Estate Without Losing Your Camisa*, I am confident that Scott's dedication to doing what's best for his clients will be invaluable in helping anyone who has a serious interest in Costa Rica real estate investments. If you are thinking of buying Costa Rica real estate, I have just three words of advice for you, "Listen to him!"
–Federico Carrillo, Minister of Finance for Costa Rica, former CEO, Bolsa Nacional de Valores (BNV) (the largest Stock Exchange in Central America) and former senior vice president of Lehman Brothers in New York.

I am pleased to recommend *How To Buy Costa Rica Real Estate Without Losing Your Camisa* written by Scott Oliver. I have known Scott for some years now and he has been thorough in his research of Costa Rican real estate issues. His concern about the lack of information for real estate purchasers in Costa Rica prompted him to write this *unique* book, which will educate and protect people who wish to purchase real estate in Costa Rica."
–Roger A. Petersen, attorney and author of *The Legal Guide To Costa Rica*.

Even if you are only remotely interested in buying, renting or investing in Costa Rica real estate, this is a *must-read* book. If you are serious about it, this book will become your bible!
-Kevin C. Myers, author of the best-selling real estate book, *Buy It, Fix It, Sell It – Profit!*

ACKNOWLEDGEMENTS

Acknowledgements go to my contributing editor, Vicky Longland, who has spent her adult life in several Latin American countries working with human-development agencies and later as a translator and writer. Her insights into the realities of Latin culture and business come from living and working closely with the people. She oversaw the building of three homes in Ecuador and has used the experience to provide firsthand input into this edition of 'How To Buy Costa Rica Real Estate Without Losing Your Camisa'.

I applaud Ned Brantly's excellent photos, Barbara Adams' patient proofreading and editing. My thanks also go to all who contributed their expertise: Randy Berg, Federico Carillo-Zurcher, Susan Carmichael, David Garrett, Daveed Hollander, Ginette Laurin, Eric Liljenstolpe, George Lundquist, Scott MacDougal, Glenn Mather, Russ Martin, Jere McKinney, Terry Mills, Kathy Oconitrillo, Roger Petersen, Richard Philps, Manuel Pinto, Elias Robles, Jerry and Ana Werth, plus everyone who has clicked onto **WeLoveCostaRica.com** and provided their own invaluable feedback.

CONTENTS

INTRODUCTION

What This Book Will Do For You

This is not a book about living in Costa Rica; it is a comprehensive English-language guide to buying Costa Rica real estate.

When you search for suitable Costa Rica real estate, whether it is to live in full time, as a holiday home or as an investment, you need to be well informed about **the challenges** of Costa Rica real estate:

- Contrary to what some people may have told you, **there is no Multiple Listing Service** to speak of, so trying to establish even a rough idea of what a piece of property is worth is extremely difficult. Take a look on the internet and you will often find the **exact same property** listed by different 'brokers' at **dramatically different prices**.

- Half the population of Costa Rica call themselves 'brokers' because any Tom, Dick or José can freely call themselves a real estate 'broker'. To be involved with Costa Rica real estate, **you do not need any qualifications**, training or experience whatsoever to call yourself a 'broker'.

- An organization of real estate brokers does exist; however, very few people who call themselves brokers have even heard of it, never mind belong to it, and **nobody is regulating** or monitoring these people!

- The laws governing Costa Rica real estate are based on **Napoleonic Laws** and not Common Laws as they are in the US and Canada. How much do you know about the Napoleonic Law system?

This means that when buying Costa Rica real estate which may be **one of the biggest investments** of your life. More than likely, you will be listening to **'expert' advice** coming from someone with **zero qualifications** or training in real estate, who is trying very hard to earn a sales commission selling you a property that could be **overpriced**.

If it sounds like a **recipe for disaster**, it can be!

There are a few excellent Costa Rica real estate professionals but **finding them is a challenge**. Why? Some of these professionals have so much business they don't even have a Website!

So how do you do your homework? How do you ensure that you're not going to lose your shirt (*su camisa*) or get ripped off when buying real estate here?

You could look on the internet.

Costa Rica Real Estate Information on the internet

Many people surf the Web searching for information about Costa Rica real estate and think that because it's there in writing it must be accurate. It may indeed be accurate, but you should still do your homework.

One problem facing English speakers trying to find quality homes at reasonable prices is that you are only going to notice the Costa Rica property advertisements, magazines and Websites in your own language - English!

If you search for Costa Rica real estate on Google, you will find nearly five million Websites listed! - **That's more Websites than people living here!** And how many of those sites actually have affordable Costa Rica property? - The answer is none! *Nada*!

They all want to sell you the highest priced real estate available because that means fatter commissions for them. But nobody has been focusing on helping you find quality Costa Rica homes at reasonable prices! Until now.

A fancy Website is cheap to produce and can be created in a matter of hours. For the most part you rarely know *who* is behind a Website nor how qualified they are to do what they claim they are capable of doing.

You should also remember that someone with real estate for sale, whether a professional broker or private seller, will naturally be enthusiastic about his geographical area but, is the area really suitable for you? **Only you** can determine that and you're only going to be able to verify that fact by visiting the area, not just once, but preferably a few times during the dry season as well as the rainy or 'green' season.

The internet can be a good start but until you have visited Costa Rica, you will not appreciate that even though this is a small country, the differences among areas in costs, climate, safety and accessibility can be dramatic.

Costa Rica Real Estate Information from Newspapers

You can also find some useful information in the local English-language newspaper. Some of it is good; however, if you're reading an article written by an intern making US$200 *per month*, it is doubtful that person has ever owned real estate. You might consider it useful information, but certainly not *expert* advice.

I'm not criticizing the writer for lack of experience - we all have to start somewhere - but if you are making an important decision (and buying Costa Rica real estate is definitely a big financial decision), you must find up-to-date information from **real experts** with real experience and not trainee journalists or newspapers (English or Spanish) relying on advertising revenues for survival.

Costa Rica Real Estate by the Book

Looking through Amazon.com you will see dozens of books listed under 'Costa Rica living' but none available on 'Costa Rica real estate.' The **first, most concise book available on Costa Rica real estate in English** is the one you are reading now.

Living Abroad in Costa Rica by Erin Van Rheenen is the most recently published book about **living in Costa Rica**. It's a well-researched publication that gives some **excellent advice** and does not try to sell you anything.

But some books should be read with a healthy dose of skepticism.

Various 'how-to' books about living and retiring in Central America have been written by authors who have never actually lived in those countries. The same goes for investment recommendations. One notorious 'investment program' that was recommended in a popular Costa Rica guide book was later shut down by the authorities. So you can see how you must beware of unsubstantiated 'expertise'.

Costa Rica Real Estate by Tour Guides

Let us remember that a tour guide is just that - a tour guide - and **rarely an investment expert** or a real estate expert. From the extensive research that was done for this book, it would appear that none of the tour guides have any professional real estate or investment training.

Follow the advice of 'experts' with no training or qualifications whatsoever in real estate or investments and **you may indeed 'lose your shirt'!**

So What Can You Do?

More so than in the regulated first world, here **you simply must do your homework** and only hire **trained, qualified** and **experienced** real estate and legal professionals.

In publishing this book, I do not claim to know everything about Costa Rica real estate. Nobody is that smart. My area of expertise for the last 20 years has been international investing. During that time, my international clients have invested hundreds of millions of dollars, **safely, privately, profitably** and **tax-free** in many of the world's best offshore hedge funds.

With ten years' experience on Wall Street plus nearly ten years working as an international investment advisor, I work for a few of the wealthiest people in Costa Rica. This includes the family of my friend - the Costa Rica Minister of Finance, who was kind enough to review and recommend this book.

This experience has given me access to many experts that you would never be able to find even if you lived here.

Why Is This Important to You?

It's important because **wealthy people demand** and expect the **best advice** that money can buy. It's my job to ensure my clients are given that advice from the most qualified experts available. I have personally hunted down dozens of the top experts to help my clients achieve their goals both with business, real estate, investing and in their day-to-day lives.

Even living here, **it has taken me over five years** to find the small group of truly expert real estate professionals with whom my investment clients work. Imagine how difficult it can be for someone to find a qualified professional when they don't live here. That's why **we are here to help you.**

If you are seriously interested in Costa Rica real estate and enjoying a **secure, stress-free, affordable lifestyle** then you've come to the right place.

Simply put, my goal in both writing this book and creating my Website at **WeLoveCostaRica.com** is **to help you!** I want to help **educate and protect** you who have a sincere desire to know more about Costa Rica real estate and to provide you with objective, non-commercial *expert* information.

There is also no advertising of any kind in this book.

My mission is to give you the right contacts and objective, expert information to enable you to enjoy living in Costa Rica the way you've always dreamed of. You may even decide to live here today and not just when you retire!

If you insist on the best and want to work with **qualified, experienced, trustworthy, reference-checked and personally, highly-recommended** real estate professionals, then please visit **WeLoveCostaRica.com** and click on **'Help-U-Search'.**

What's In It for Us?

When a wealthy investor comes to me looking for advice and my connections to some of the world's best hedge funds, my colleagues in Zurich, London, Dublin or Hong Kong and I carefully analyze the investment objectives and make what we consider to be the most appropriate recommendation. Our client then invests his money.

These high-probability, low-risk investment recommendations are where we feel the opportunity for growth is significant yet the overall risk is limited…

We are doing the exact same thing with Costa Rica real estate. When you make the decision to buy Costa Rica real estate, we are hoping that you will give us an opportunity to help you because:

- we will **help you to clearly define** exactly what type of property you are searching for;

- with the enormous amount of valuable information you find on our Website at **WeLoveCostaRica.com**, you will know where the **current Costa Rica real estate opportunities** are;

- if you are searching for affordable Costa Rica real estate, you'll quickly notice that we are your *only* source for quality, affordable homes for around US$100K. We also have excellent connections to help you find your new luxury home in Costa Rica;

- we will help you pinpoint the **most suitable geographical location** for you and your family;

- we will recommend the **best real estate and legal professionals** to ensure that everything is done quickly, efficiently and painlessly!

- this will **save you significant time** and money by only showing you the most appropriate properties and ensuring that you are working with **honest, experienced, qualified brokers** who have your best interests at heart.

If high-probability, low-risk real estate investment is what interests you, please visit **WeLoveCostaRica.com** and then click on '**Help-U-Search**'.

S.O.

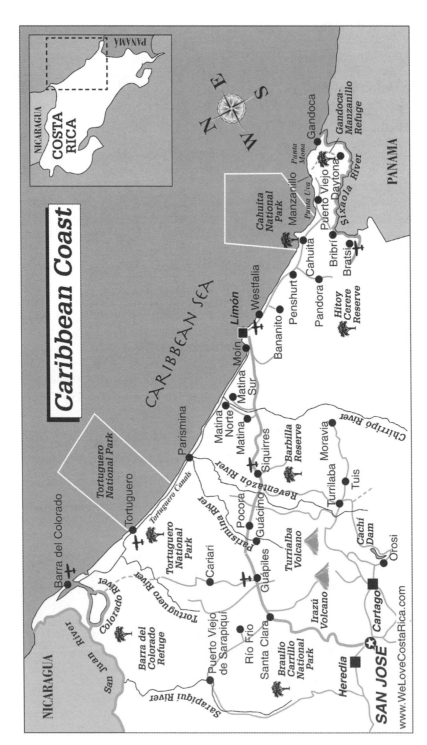

Caribbean Coast

www.WeLoveCostaRica.com

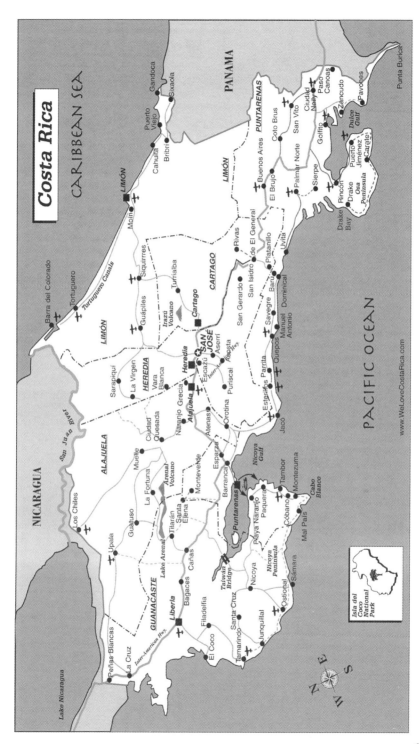

Costa Rica

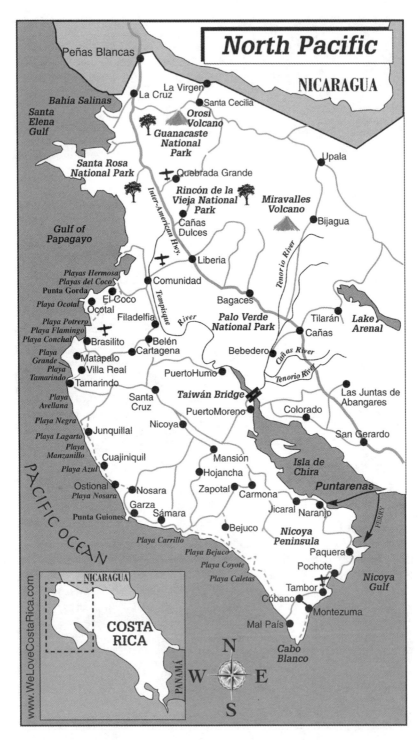

North Pacific

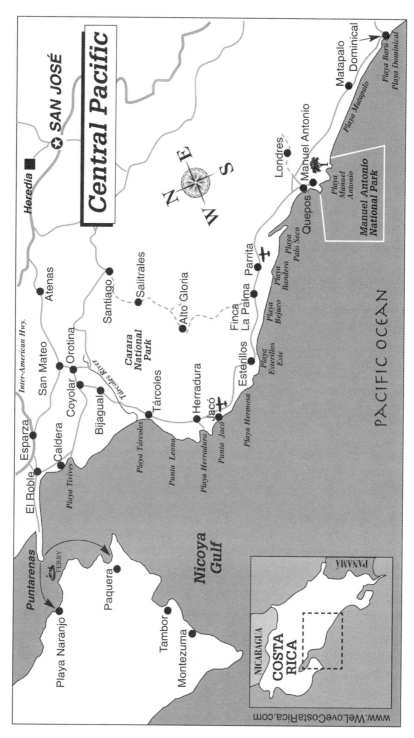

Central Pacific

SAN JOSÉ

Heredia

PACIFIC OCEAN

Manuel Antonio National Park

www.WeLoveCostaRica.com

17

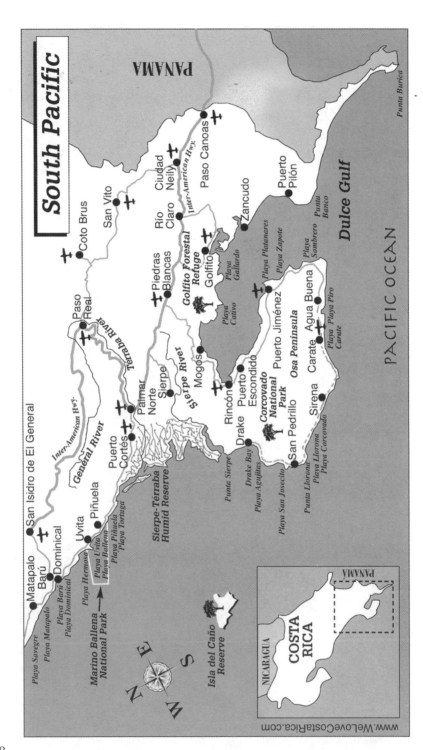

South Pacific

PANAMA

Punta Burica

Dulce Gulf

PACIFIC OCEAN

Paso Canoas

Ciudad Neily

Río Claro

Coto Brus

San Vito

Zancudo

Puerto Pilón

Piedras Blancas

Golfito Forestal Refuge

Golfito

Playa Gallardo

Playa Platanares

Playa Zapote

Playa Sombrero

Punta Banco

Paso Real

Inter-American Hwy.

Playa Cativo

Puerto Jiménez

Agua Buena

Playa Piro

Playa Carate

Térraba River

Sierpe River

Mogos

Rincón

Puerto Escondido

Osa Peninsula

Carate

Palmar Norte

Sierpe

Drake

Drake Bay

Corcovado National Park

Sirena

San Pedrillo

Punta Sierpe

Playa Aguilas

Playa San Josecito

Punta Llorona

Playa Llorona

Playa Corcovado

Puerto Cortés

General River

Inter-American Hwy.

San Isidro de El General

Matapalo Barú

Dominical

Uvita

Piñuela

Playa Savegre

Playa Matapalo

Playa Barú Dominical

Playa Hermosa

Playa Piñuela Playa Tortuga

Playa Uvita Playa Ballena

Marino Ballena National Park

Sierpe-Térraba Humid Reserve

Isla del Caño Reserve

N E S W

NICARAGUA

COSTA RICA

PANAMA

www.WeLoveCostaRica.com

18

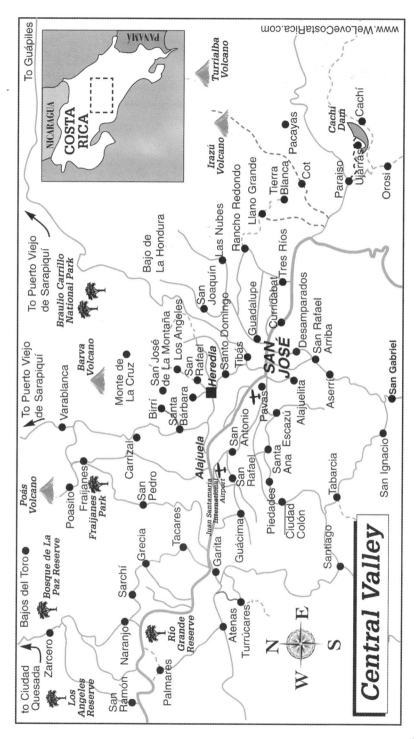

Central Valley

19

Chapter One

Welcome

Costa Rica welcomes you!

This is no idle promise. This tiny Central American nation can become the place you call home as it is for many other expatriates searching for their slice of Paradise.

You've probably seen the TV documentaries extolling its natural wonders, peaceful traditions and friendly citizens, and maybe you have even spent a few days vacation in the past. So is it crossing your mind to dig a little deeper? Whatever your reasons may be, perhaps you have already started doing some research on Costa Rica as a place to move to permanently.

Where do you go to find out about the ideal home or piece of property for you, with all the ins and outs explained, all the steps you have to take with all those hidden potholes revealed that can bring an unwary buyer down? Right here!

The *How To Buy Costa Rica Real Estate Without Losing Your Camisa* book is just that. It is a comprehensive step-by-step guide book **prepared for you by the many experts** from **WeLoveCostaRica.com,** based on the kind of experience that only comes from living in the country, speaking the local language and building up the contacts of professionals to give you the quality, professionally endorsed information you need.

> Half the population of Costa Rica seems to work as brokers because any Tom, Dick or José can freely call themselves a real estate 'broker.' To be involved with Costa Rica real estate, you do not need any qualifications, training or experience whatsoever to call yourself a 'broker' and there is nobody monitoring the people that do.

Why Move To Costa Rica?

It is easier to ask, "Why not?" This **peace-loving country** filled with stunning scenery, sunshine and smiles has plenty going for it, making it a major magnet for tourists and an equally attractive destination for foreigners looking for a **safe, friendly, affordable** haven to settle in.

Some Statistics And Facts

Costa Rica's land area is 50,660 km2, just a bit smaller than West Virginia. Bordered by Panama to the south-east, Nicaragua on its north-western border and the Caribbean and Pacific Ocean on either side, it forms part of the isthmus of Central America.

With 1,290 km (800 miles) of coastline, beautiful sandy beaches are not in short supply and by law all are freely accessible to the public. The interior offers landscapes as varied as coffee plantations, rain forests, steaming volcanoes and grassy flatlands.

Two main seasons apply to most of the country if not quite at the same times of year. Dry season runs from December to April and rainy from May to November although the Caribbean side has an overall wetter climate with its driest season in September and October.

The climate and temperature levels are in fact determined more by elevation, from tropical heat and humidity at sea level to cooler sub-tropical temperatures in the mountains.

In Costa Rica real estate, there is no Multiple Listing Service to speak of so trying to establish even a rough idea of what a piece of property is worth is extremely difficult. Take a look on the internet and you will often find the exact same property listed by different brokers at dramatically different prices.

The fertile Central Valley at an altitude of about 1,000 meters (3,280 feet) is home to most of the population, centered around the capital, San José, and the three other major towns of Cartago, Alajuela and Heredia. The temperatures here stay around 21 - 24° C 69.8 – 75°F), while on the coasts they can reach a steamy 32° C (89.6°F) although the Pacific coast tends to be somewhat hotter than the Caribbean.

The two coasts are separated by four small but distinct mountain ranges of both uplifted mountains and over 100 volcano cones, seven of which are active. From the capital, San José, you can see four of the major volcanoes: Poas, Barva, Irazú and Turrialba, and they add a dramatic backdrop to any picture window.

These volatile peaks are part of the "Rim of Fire" around the Pacific Basin although volcanic activity has been quiet in recent years with the last eruption (of Irazú), spewing out ash over San José back in 1963. The highest peak, Chirripó, at 3,810 m is not a volcano but part of the geological uplift that created the Talamanca mountain range stretching down into Panama.

Almost four million people live in Costa Rica and the **high standard of living** is reflected in part by their average life expectancy of 76.6 years. The people are known for their **friendliness to foreigners,** their tolerance and commitment to compromise and peace. Costa Ricans (or *Ticos* as they call themselves) do not like confrontation and will go to lengths to avoid a show-down.

Costa Rica has been **independent since 1821** and has the longest democracy in the region, established in 1949 when it abolished its armed forces and the military. As a republic, it has three governing branches: legislative with a single chamber of *diputados* or deputies who meet in the Legislative Assembly; executive presided by the President and the cabinet in the *Consejo de Gobierno,* and judicial. Elections are held every four years for President, Congress members and local municipal representatives.

The police force is armed and fulfils several of the duties that would normally fall under the military coming either under the urban-based Civil Guard or the Rural Assistance Guard. Sub-divisions cover other units such as the Coast Guard, traffic police, the Presidential Guard and Municipal Police.

It is a fallacy to assume that the lack of a military means no gun-toting officials or special forces in military-style uniforms. What it does mean is the millions of dollars that might go on defense expenditure can be spent on education and health budgets instead, and this can be seen with its enviably high standards in both areas as compared to the rest of the region.

Costa Rica has a **relatively stable economy** based on agriculture (bananas and coffee), tourism and the soft technology and food processing industries.

Intel, Procter & Gamble, Glaxo SmithKline, Motorola, LL Bean, Align Technologies, Abbott Labs, Baxter Healthcare, Roche & Pfizer, Western Union and many others have all made huge commitments to the country and assert their satisfaction with the quality and education of the local workforce. With literacy running at 96% of the whole population, that is no hasty compliment.

Communications and internet systems have improved over the past three years and cellular phones are in high demand, which lead to temporary shortages of lines. Cable television or DirecTV reach most areas of Costa Rica. The country is served by major international airlines and a good, and very affordable overland bus service operates throughout the country. International buses (TicaBus and NicaBus) travel to the rest of Central America.

Quick And Easy To Reach

Access to Costa Rica has never been easier. The country is now serviced by two international airports: Juan Santamaría for San José and the Central Valley, and Daniel Oduber in Liberia opening up the whole Guanacaste and northern regions.

If you are coming from (and this is by no means the complete list): Miami, New York, Houston, Atlanta, Washington, Madrid, Los Angeles, Amsterdam, Pittsburg, Phoenix, Barcelona, Mexico City, Charlotte or Fort Lauderdale, you can get a direct flight straight into San José!

Continental, Delta, American Airlines and United now fly into the Liberia international airport. And just in case you care about which company flies you here, you have a choice from: American Airlines, Delta, Continental, United, Iberia, LKM, Grupo Taca, Cubana, Avianca, Mexicana, Air Madrid, Lacsa, Martin Air, Air Canada US Airways, American West Airlines and BWIA.

Costa Rica to Miami takes just over three hours; from Atlanta nearly four hours, these being the closest hubs - now that's a short hop to reach Paradise!

A Few Disadvantages

Yes, even in this haven there are a few. Flooding in low-lying areas can wash out roads and shut down electricity and telephone services, especially along the coast; occasional earthquakes cause your crockery to rattle such as the November 2004 earthquake measuring 6.2 on the Richter scale; hurricane backlash on the Caribbean coast brings torrential rains (but great surfing!) and volcanic eruptions have made themselves felt in the past, mostly with ash blown out over cities and farmland.

There have been outbreaks of dengue fever but it is very unlikely that you will experience tropical diseases in Costa Rica, which prides itself on supplying **safe piped drinking water** to its people and offering an unparalleled health care service.

Becoming An Expatriate In Costa Rica

According to the Costa Rica Chamber of Real Estate Brokers (*Camera Costarricense de Corredores de Bienes Raices*), Costa Rica is ranked fourth as being an ideal country for foreign investment because there are so few restrictions on foreigners owning property here. Even if you come in with your tourist visa, you have just about the same rights as *Ticos*.

Many people (some 35,000 North Americans alone, not to mention Canadians, Europeans and other Latin Americans) have gone before you and **live here happily** as retirees, self-employed entrepreneurs or contracted employees.

Not all of them have bought into real estate; many rent, but unless they have been spoon-fed by their employers and handed the keys of a house ready to move into, they, like most of us, will have had to face the challenge of finding a property on their own or through a broker.

There is an organization of brokers involved with Costa Rica real estate; however, very few people who call themselves 'brokers' have even heard of it never mind belong to it. And although it is lobbying for government endorsement, nobody is currently regulating its members!

So let's say you have made that commitment to move to Costa Rica; you now need somewhere to live. Buying a house or getting into commercial property is going to be one of your biggest investments and greatest challenges. You are going to put out your valuable savings or hard-earned cash or scrape up a loan somehow so you need to get it right - first time.

What Major Hurdles Will You Face?

First of all, **stop thinking like a gringo!** That's meant in the nicest possible way, but do not expect to go about finding property as you would in North America or Europe. Let's just go over some of the realities you will face in Costa Rica:

- The Costa Rica real estate market has **no real Multiple Listing Service as such.** If you go on the internet to research houses, you may find the same property listed by different brokers at alarmingly different prices. It can be hard to get even a rough idea of how much a property is worth.

- Anyone can set themselves up as a broker and after a few days traveling around you will meet any number. They seem to grow in Costa Rica's lush forests, there are so many, but do they know what they are doing? Not necessarily; **no qualifications or training are needed** here to call yourself a broker.

- There is a non-governmental, voluntary association of brokers involved with Costa Rica real estate: the Costa Rican Chamber of Real Estate Brokers (*Camera Costarricense de Corredores de Bienes Raices - CCCBR*).

  In spite of its efforts to make the industry more professional and responsible, even this association has no legally binding statutes to which it must adhere. **You have no recourse** should your broker turn out to be incompetent or worse, a fraud out for the highest possible sales commission without providing the service.

- Are you familiar with Costa Rica law, which is based on Napoleonic (Civil) Law, not Common Law as used in Canada and the US?

- **Do you speak fluent Spanish** to be able to decipher it and all the municipal bylaws that may apply wherever you choose to move?

  If you are coming from Canada or the US, there is no need to worry about electrical differences – there are none. You can use the same appliances in Costa Rica that you use in the US and Canada.

There is no doubt that Costa Rica is booming and real estate prices in certain areas have rocketed. If you know where to look and who to talk to, however, bargains can be found and the choice is wide. **Now is definitely the time to consider buying.**

Think about this! In the next two decades, more than 70 million Americans will be retiring and looking for suitable and attractive retirement property, and that doesn't mean just within the US. This early wave of pensioned-off Baby Boomers think mobile and will be turning their sights all over the globe.

That means real estate in Costa Rica could well be a timely and **possibly a high-profit investment** opportunity, if you act promptly. You will be making a good investment – **if you get the right help.** So where do you find this help?

Right here, with the ***How To Buy Costa Rica Real Estate Without Losing Your Camisa***. We can give you the sort of inside information that normally only Costa Ricans or well-connected long-term residents find.

You will be able to **contact trustworthy professionals** who speak English and you will have access to our carefully built-up portfolio of real estate contacts. The *How To Buy Costa Rica Real Estate Without Losing Your Camisa* book is your invaluable tool to a successful, **hassle-free** property purchase.

Why must anyone with substantial assets have some of their liquid assets invested offshore? You can learn more by reading our articles at **WeLoveCostaRica.com**

It's Not Like Back Home

Back home you can cruise the real estate agents and pick up listings of areas that interest you, buy a national or local newspaper to spend time on some do-it-yourself searching or get on the books of a few brokers.

You can go online and sort through listings without even getting in your car. Because of Multiple Listing Services (MSL), you will have a reasonable idea what property is worth in any area with attractive photos and floor plans to give you the picture.

According to the US Census Bureau, over the next 10 years, the number of Americans turning 65 each year is expected to jump 73%, to 3.95 million in 2011 from 2.07 million in 2001. A huge and increasing number of people from Latin America and Europe are also coming to Costa Rica. With these demographics, it's going to get busier here.

Back home you wouldn't bother (or dare) to ask that broker whether he or she was qualified to do the job, would you? You naturally expect them to work hard on your behalf to help find you a good property - the kind you want, not the kind they want to sell for more commission.

You assume they will help you get the best deal, efficiently explain all the legal transactions and paperwork involved and help you close the deal with minimum fuss.

Things down in Costa Rica are a bit different and that is one of the most important lessons you will learn if you decide to buy property. You need to be able to get underneath the many glossy ads promising *heaven-on-earth* properties that also come with sky-high prices. And you need to find a broker who will work with you, **efficiently, professionally and in a language you can easily understand.**

Want to know more about the Costa Rica Cost of Living? After spending a month 'in the field', author Vicky Longland reports on hundreds of prices of everyday items that most expatriates look for in Costa Rica stores. Registered VIP Members of **WeLoveCostaRica.com** can find this in the Downloads section.

Is Costa Rica A Safe Place To Buy Real Estate?

Why not find out firsthand from Susan Carmichael, author of *Crime In Costa Rica* and regular contributor to **WeLoveCostaRica.com**

We live in a world where a butter knife and nail clippers are considered weapons on airplanes; bombs are hidden in shoes and inside people's bodies; prisons are overcrowded; trains are blown up; children are gunned down in schools. **Is it safe in paradise?**

When I first traveled to Costa Rica, I walked through downtown like an innocent tourist high on paradise air. Lee Weiler of the Don Carlos Hotel explained to me some visitors leave all common sense behind because they are *traveling to paradise*. They walk downtown with their wallet hanging out of their pocket. "We have criminals here," he said. "If we didn't, they'd import them from Miami." I had always kept my wits about me and my guard up when I traveled in New York, but getting to know the people of Costa Rica I thought was like petting a puppy—each person seemed so gentle and harmless. I learned, as in any other city, to **stay aware and travel smart.**

The subject of security, whether on a personal or a national level, is complex. **Different neighborhoods experience different crime rates.** Tourist and resident will be faced with varying degrees of crime and aggression, especially in large cities.

In 2004, the preliminary numbers show crime rates declining in Costa Rica. Even as violence and terror scrape away at Costa Rica's tradition of pacifism and peace, this small country remains **a safe place** to hang your *sombrero*. Compared to the following countries, Costa Rica ranked low in the number of assaults per 1,000 people: United States reported 7.98; United Kingdom had 7.54; Canada 7.32; Chile 7.32; Germany 1.4; Japan .34; and Costa Rica reported 0.19 for the same time period.

Robberies continue to be one of Costa Rica's biggest crime concerns. Here's how those same countries compared: Chile reported 7.14 robberies per 1,000; Costa Rica 5.02; United Kingdom 1.59; United States 1.46; Canada 0.85; Germany 0.71; and Japan was last with 0.04 robberies per 1,000 people. (Data supplied by *Seventh United Nations Survey of Crime Trends and Operations of Criminal Justice* for the period 1998-2000).

My mother, about to depart on her second trip to Costa Rica just after several murders occurred in the country that made international headlines, told me many of her friends were worried for her safety because she was traveling to such a dangerous place. She explained to her friends she felt **safer in Costa Rica** than in downtown Minneapolis, Minnesota and as safe living in or visiting any other city in the United States.

I got curious. How did Costa Rica, specifically San José, stack up against other major US cities with comparable populations between 300,000 and 450,000 in murders per 100,000 people? San José's population is around 400,000.

I picked four other cities scattered throughout the US for comparison. Guess what? San José came in last. In the year 2002, Kansas City, Missouri reported 18.5 murders; Minneapolis, Minnesota had 12; Tampa, Florida and Sacramento, California were almost even with 11.7 and 11.1 respectively; San José, Costa Rica ranked far below the other cities with 6.4.

The Cantón Central, which is the greater metropolitan area of San José, Costa Rica, still ranked below all four cities in the US listed above for murders with 10.7 per 100,000. (Data for Costa Rica from **www.poder-judicial.go.cr** which is the government's data resource. Data for the United States from **www.city-data.com)**

My family rented for three years before buying a home in Costa Rica. We wanted to sample different neighborhoods. Our first home was in downtown San José. We shipped into the country a used car, a load of appliances, a television, stereo, pots and pans—the basic essentials of modern life. It was enough to attract attention because even though it looked like basic stuff to us, it made us seem like wealthy immigrants to the locals. In Costa Rica, gringos are perceived as a prosperous group. Basically, this is true. We do have more money than most Costa Ricans (yet less than the families who inherited fortunes from coffee estates!). Costa Rica's poverty rate hovers around 20%; **a typical family makes from US$400- 600 a month.** A college graduate, at a top-paying job (after a few years of experience), may earn US$1,000 per month.

When I walked downtown, vendors heckled me: "Hey blue eyes! Good buy!" They learned a few key English words and assumed because of my Caucasian looks I had loads of money flapping out of my back pocket or hidden in my socks burning to be spent on lottery tickets, cheap nail polish, mops or ceramic pigs.

Even though Costa Rica suffers from poverty, the country continues to maintain a **relative social prosperity** in a historically poor region. Tips on safe travel will help you navigate the country for several weeks, but successfully living in Costa Rica **requires an awareness of culture and history**, along with social and economic issues.

Relocating a family or retiring in a different country is an enormous undertaking. Without understanding some basic differences in culture, the transition to Latin America can be frustrating and stress-provoking. A lack of cultural understanding can stereotype a society as being more violent, crime-ridden or exasperating than it is in reality. When I moved to Costa Rica, I dismissed the cultural differences - didn't think much about it - but they are always there.

A good deal in real estate may be a bad idea for your family's safety or your pocketbook in the long run. Living in upscale neighborhoods, however, will not isolate anyone from crime. Crooks gather where fortunes hide. A level head, cultural awareness, a good real estate agent who'll inform you of the reality of the location - blemishes and all (heck, nothing's perfect) and a balanced diet (well, it can't hurt) may keep your family safe and your appliances plugged in to your own wall.

Guns, dogs, gates, guards, someone always in the home and now electronic security systems are Costa Rica's way of deterring crime. Self-protection is an accepted cultural norm in Costa Rica as all of Latin America. A majority of homes have high gates topped by razor wire, cemented-in broken glass or decorative metal spikes. At first, the number of guns and gates can seem oppressive. However, in a society where the police force is poorly funded, it is the norm to try to out-think the criminal with what may seem radical means to those unaccustomed to the practice. Of course, these methods are not always successful. Yet most businesses and homes feel more secure with one or more of them in place.

In the building boom in the suburbs of Costa Rica, many new urbanizations west and east of San José are choosing 24-hour (often armed) guards at the entrance instead of barred windows, tall gates or barbed wire. Though some residents still swear to the effectiveness of barred windows, many homes are being built with tall, clear windows free of unsightly bars.

Now that I'm living in a suburban setting, we have a tall boundary wall with a single entry gate surrounding the property, but no bars. We bought an alarm system at the mall but one drawback of such security systems is that the home base, which reacts to a crime situation or emergency, may be miles away. One of the best features of the alarm systems for me is the plaque installed on the front gate. Since alarm companies are so new to Costa Rica,

I'm hoping thieves may view the house as too problematical and move on.

We never have security alerts in Costa Rica. Each sunny day arrives and people go about living. I watch my daughter grow up in this developing country and I question why Costa Rica would ever want to catch up to the dicey world of split atoms and Patriot Acts. The leaders of Costa Rica, as a matter of policy, choose peace over weapons. Even with the current political uproar in 2004-2005 involving former Costa Rican presidents (note the plural!) milking contracts for their own bank accounts, the people of the country remain committed, and possibly more resolved, to a **peaceful existence.**

Maybe the first thing you will think of when you set foot on Costa Rican soil is not one of worry or dread, but rather one of **peace and tranquility**. Maybe you will find a sliver of paradise after all.

Our thanks to Susan Carmichael, a freelance writer living in Costa Rica for her in-depth crime research. Register at **WeLoveCostaRica.com** and read more of her fascinating articles about living in Costa Rica or visit Susan's site at **motherjungle.com**

Your Living Needs And Preferences

Before even stepping outside and using up your time and energy visiting properties at random, sit down and try to think carefully about your needs and expectations. Take a look at the checklist below and answer them carefully and honestly.

These are the types of questions we ask at **WeLoveCostaRica.com** because this information will help you to understand that there are specific, unique challenges associated with buying real estate in Costa Rica.

1. Have you been to Costa Rica before?
2. Please rate your **Spanish speaking skills,** if any?
3. Can you give a detailed idea of what type of home you're looking for? Number of bedrooms? Bathrooms? Free-standing family home? Apartment? Condo? Lot size? Garden? Farm?
4. Does the property need to be on one level only or can it have more?
5. **How much land** would you prefer to have as part of the property?
6. At what temperature would you need to turn on the air conditioning? And at what temperature would you turn on the heating? What is the ideal temperature for you?
7. Do you have **pets** that will be here with you in Costa Rica? What kind of pets?

8. Are you single or coming with a partner?
9. **Do you have children** with you? If so, what ages?
10. Do you spend a lot of time online?
11. What hobbies and or interests are important to you?
12. Would you like to live on a golf course?
13. Are there any **special medical requirements** or disabilities that need to be taken into consideration?
14. How far (in time) would you be willing to travel to buy your groceries and supplies?
15. How far (in time) would you be willing to go to the nearest international airport?
16. Would you prefer to live near a Catholic Church or Temple? Is that important to you?
17. How soon would you prefer to move into your new home? How long are you prepared to wait before moving into a new home?
18. Is this a property that you will live in full time or only part time?
19. Will you be completely retired? Or are you planning to work or start a business?
20. Do you know which specific geographical areas that interest you? (Remember that Costa Rica has a Pacific as well as a Caribbean coast.)
21. If you found your ideal property, **how much exactly** have you set aside to buy the property?
22. Have you already hired a Costa Rican attorney to help you with any legal, residency or real estate matters?
23. Is there any additional information that's important for you to remember?

Thanks to the wonderful weather here, many older houses in Costa Rica do not have hot water. Sorry to state the obvious but if you need it, make sure that your potential home does indeed have hot water.

And you remember that **the laws here are based on Napoleonic Laws** and not Common Laws as they are in the US and Canada, right?

We feel this information:

- helps us **clearly define** exactly what type of property you are looking for;
- helps pinpoint the **most suitable** geographical location for you and your family;
- allows us to recommend the **best possible real estate professionals** in that area

As I hope you will see, we at **WeLoveCostaRica.com** plan on guiding you in the right direction. This should **save you significant time** and **money** by making sure you are only shown the most appropriate properties and making sure you are working with honest, experienced, qualified brokers.

Affordable Real Estate – Homes Under US$100K

Real estate in Costa Rica is a *hot topic*. Many people meet with a broker who insists on showing them expensive homes and apartments in the most expensive areas so the visitor goes back home **thinking that real estate in Costa Rica is expensive**. **Wrong!**

I know many people that have bought real estate in Costa Rica **(or built their own very comfortable homes) for under US$100K** and they're delighted. Their property may not be in the most exclusive areas of the country but is your own home located in *the* most exclusive area? Or do you perhaps live in a typical middle class area like most of us?

According to a Household Survey taken by the National Statistics and Census Institute (INEC), the average income of a **household** in the **richest fifth** of the population is US$1,450 per month so there's obviously a huge selection of real estate in Costa Rica being built specifically to cater to those homebuyers with that budget in mind.

If I were to come to your home town and meet with the broker who had all the fancy advertising in your area, **I would probably end up buying a more expensive** piece of property than if I had sat down with you as my friend and asked for your help in finding a great property, wouldn't I?

The same applies to real estate in Costa Rica.

Why? Because in your home town **you're not trying to sell me anything**, yet you have the intimate, real-life *insider* knowledge about your area that I need. **You know the best,** most affordable developments, the most romantic restaurant that you and your partner always go to on your anniversary and you know all about the schools, the doctors, the shops etc. You are helping me as a friend and not expecting anything in return!

That's my job too! I'm your *amigo* in Costa Rica. **I'm here to help educate and protect you** so that you make an informed decision about property in this country so you can listen to me with confidence.

As far as property in this country is concerned, I would strongly recommend that **you rent** for at least six months **before you buy a property anywhere**. This one simple piece of advice has probably saved people millions of dollars.

I am not a real estate broker; I have no burning desire to sell you anything and already make a great living so I don't mind if you never buy anything from me. However, **I do mind** if you make a poor decision because of bad advice and then end up unhappy and blame Costa Rica.

But Where Do You Find the Affordable Properties?

La Nación (**nacion.com**) is by far the biggest and most influential Spanish language newspaper in Costa Rica and on Saturday, various real estate projects are detailed in a supplement which is called *Metro Cuadrado - M2*. You can find dozens of display advertisements and hundreds of classified ads listed.

Here's just one great example for you. One Saturday, we carefully examined all the classified advertisements for **houses** and **condos for sale** in both *La Nación* as well as *The Tico Times*.

Obviously the advertising in *La Nación* is targeting Spanish-speaking readers in Costa Rica and the advertising in *The Tico Times* is aimed at English speakers.

Here is what we discovered:

- *La Nación* - **59%** of the classified advertisements were for properties under US$100K and the average sales price = US$91K

- *The Tico Times* - **20%** of the classified advertisements were for properties below US$100K and the average sales price = US$125K

That's a dramatic difference and it clearly shows the different target market that each newspaper's advertising is trying to reach.

We should remember that only the most *adventurous* gringos would want to live in some of these areas. However, we also know gringos who have bought homes for far less than US$100K and are quite happily living in a *Tico* area in a *Tico*-style home.

Want To See Some Tico Homes For Yourself? Online?

If you would like to do your own online research and see some of the Tico Websites that feature **homes under US$100K** then stay with us…

Some of these homes may be no more than a simple, concrete box but you have to start somewhere. These properties have only been seen in the newspaper; I have not visited them so *cannot* personally recommend any of these developments. However, they are all **brand new homes** and some of them have been built by very reputable Costa Rica construction companies.

There are **thousands of properties for sale** and you'll be able to see many listed in *La Nación* and in the classified section of their Website (**www.economicos.com/navigate.do**) but here's a handful of examples in and around San José for you.

As you can see though, not all these real estate developers have Websites:

1. Apartments in Santa Ana at *Casa del Sol* (proyectourbano.net) from US$70K
2. Homes in Belén - *El Paso de las Garzas* starting at US$80K
3. Loft-type townhouses **(dhcsoluciones.com)** in Curridabat from US$60K
4. Homes from US$44K in San Francisco de Heredia **(constancia.co.cr)**
5. Apartments near Hotel Irazú in San Jose starting at US$85K
6. *La Plantación* homes (**piacacr.com**) in Heredia from US$55K
7. *Condominio Guaria Blanca* homes in Heredia from US$80K
8. Homes in San Joaquín de Flores from US$90K
9. Homes in Heredia **(dulillyana.com)** from about US$50K
10. *Residencial Milenio* homes in Heredia from US$50K
11. *Valle Arriba* condominiums in Escazú from US$85K
12. *Brisas del Oeste* **(brisasdeloeste.com)** apartments in San Jose from US$75K
13. *Santillana del Mar* **(residenciaselegantes.com/santillana.htm)** homes in Heredia from US$66K
14. *Villa Luisiana* **(fomentourbano.co.cr)** homes in Heredia from US$100K
15. Homes at *Montelindo Residencial* **(fomentourbano.co.cr)** in Moravia from US$50K
16. *Las Flores* 155 m2 (1,667 ft2) of construction from US$83K
17. Apartments in Escazú **(milano.co.cr/general-eng.html)** from US$100K
18. *Cala de Belén* homes from US$92K
19. *Residencias Cibeles* in San Isidro de Heredia from US$95K
20. *Residencial Jerez* in Heredia **(constancia.co.cr)** from US$54K
21. *Residencial Flor Natalia* from US$97K
22. *Calle Colonial* from US$84K
23. *Residencial Quizarco* from US$88K
24. *Condominio Zenit* in Moravia (San José) from US$100K

25. *Cataluna* homes **(residenciaselegantes.com/cataluna.htm)** from US$38K
26. *Puente de Piedra* from US$68K
27. *La Plantación* in San Roque de Barva from US$48K
28. *Villa de la Rambla* **(dhcsoluciones.com)** in Belén from US$105K
29. *Torres de la Colina* **(torresdelacolina.com/eng/)** en Escazú from US$68K
30. *Condado del Palacio* in San José - Condominiums from US$68K
31. *Condominio Campo Real* **(concasa.com)** from US$42K
32. *Residencial Puente de Piedra* in Heredia **(robleguaria.com)** from US$70K

The **big problem you face** as an English-speaking real estate buyer in Costa Rica trying to find good quality **homes under US$100K** is that you are understandably only going to notice the real estate advertisements, magazines and Websites in your own language – English!

You can just imagine how challenging it would be for a person speaking only Spanish who moves to England and then tries to understand how its system works with the goal of buying real estate. It's difficult!

Most of the Websites listed above are in Spanish only and the real estate brokers that cater to that market are primarily Spanish-speaking brokers. Unfortunately, the **English-speaking brokers really don't want** to show you *affordable* homes because their commission becomes a little 'economical.'

So What Can You Do?

You don't need any Spanish-speaking skills to just look at a home for sale. What you could do is to hire a driver by the day to take you around to various properties you wish to see. They are easy to find, cheap and most of them speak passable English. Remember that any driver or guide you meet will probably also claim to be a professional real estate broker! So when he tells you his grandfather has a great property for sale that you "must see", take everything he says with a big pinch of salt.

If you do see a property for sale that you really like (and many of the developments listed above will have a Sales Office), you can proceed to the chapter **The Purchase Process**. However, we still strongly recommend that you read every other chapter too so that you can be sure **you are making the best decision** for your needs and interests.

Affordable Homes In Costa Rica - George Lundquist's Story.

George Lundquist is the founder of *Costa Rica Retire on Social Security* and offers his personal experiences here of how he found his dream home.

Most people who visit Costa Rica promise to return and some even return to live at least part of the year. This is a result of the spectacular scenery, incredible climates, great food (including the basic food groups: beer, ice cream, and chocolate) and most of all - the Costa Rican people.

All of us who offer advice to potential buyers emphasize one important thing. **Rent for at least six months before deciding to buy**!

Nearly everyone who lives here will tell you their area is best. When this occurs ask where else they have lived and how property values and finished home prices compare (most, including people who claim to be professional brokers, really do not know).

If you can afford to live in areas that have all the amenities of the US or Canada, gated and guarded perimeters with English-speaking neighbors, there are many developers and real estate brokers who will show you a vast array of beautiful properties and homes which may seem like bargains compared to 'Up North'.

For the rest of us, however, who have a **limited amount of capital** to purchase or build a home as well as a modest retirement income there are also wonderful opportunities.

We can actually get to live in low-cost areas without all the heavy traffic, common crime and rampant snobbery that pervade the high-cost areas. There are, in fact, an **unlimited number of places** where one can buy or build a great home with electricity, phone, water, close to medical services and with fairly quick access to San Jose if it's ever required.

When we first thought of moving here and started to look at Costa Rica real estate, we decided to buy an existing house because we were totally unfamiliar with contractors, tradesmen, building codes and reliable suppliers. And our budget was limited to a **grand total of US$60,000** with which to buy a home.

We searched the internet for over one year, emailing Costa Rica real estate agents and attended seminars. We found absolutely nothing we wanted to live in at or below this price.

Then we found a home listed on the internet in our price range and went to visit it. The owners had retired from California and described the area as a place "**where you will be hugged not mugged**". They had joined the Peace Corps after retiring and were assigned to this area.

This was the first home that we bought and we were delighted with it. I can assure you there are many options to living well in Costa Rica on a modest income.

The most important aspects of living to me - climate and attitudes - are free here. And for my wife and I, all of the services such as electricity, water, gas, cell phone, internet, satellite TV, full-coverage health insurance, property taxes, garbage collection and even motorcycle insurance, the total cost is **less than US$200 per month**.

Food costs for super fresh vegetables are embarrassingly low. Supermarket eggs, chicken, seafood, hamburger (steak and roasts are not always easy to find in more rural areas), cereal and cooking supplies all cost about the same as in the US.

If you like the adventure of visiting the various farmers' markets, you will find an excellent selection of ultra-fresh fruits and vegetables at great prices.

Costa Rica houses can rent for as low as US$100 per month for an unfurnished apartment, which is obviously pretty bare, all the way up to thousands of dollars per month for huge mansions.

Remember we always recommend renting before buying. This allows you to see if you really want to live in the area. Some people are bothered by crowing roosters, barking dogs, motorcycles and other trivial but common sounds.

There are always many questions about Costa Rica medical insurance and healthcare costs. Our *Caja* (*Caja Costarricense de Seguros Sociales*) or Social Service Health Department insurance **costs less than US$25 per month** (that total is for my wife and for me - the two of us) and we are really pleased with the quality and accessibility of it.

We have used the services of private Costa Rica doctors, dentists and hospitals from time to time and are amazed at the high level of professionalism and the low cost. Our present dentist, here in Santiago de Puriscal has more modern, efficient, and painless equipment than I ever saw in the US.

In every case, we have been able to schedule an appointment within two days. So far this has included a heart specialist, an internal medicine specialist, a dentist, ophthalmologist and a pain specialist.

A typical visit to one of these Costa Rica medical professionals **costs less than US$50.** All of them can write prescriptions on the *Caja* pharmacies so the prescriptions are free. Accessibility to this service is much easier here in the rural areas than in the San José area.

When you are ready to invest in Costa Rica real estate, the question of whether it is better to build or buy an existing home must be answered. The bottom-line answer is buy an existing Costa Rica property if you can find what you want, where you want at a cost equal to or less than building.

Buy Land And Build Your Own Home?

You could do what we are now doing and buy some land to build your own home.

We are building ours near Puriscal, which is a small town west of San José. Our new home will be located on about half an acre in a community with five other like-minded people who will also have half-acre lots. We will have underground utilities, remote control front gate, central drive of concrete pavers, a horizon lap pool, an eight-foot-diameter hot tub, a one-acre park with BBQ area. All lots will be partially landscaped and we'll have a full time gardener to look after the property.

Our home will have teak ceilings, solar heated water, solid teak doors, wired for surround sound, granite counter tops, custom wood cabinets and include refrigerator, stove with extractor hood, dishwasher and a large washing machine and dryer.

We will be less than 1 km (.62 mile) to basic supplies and less than 45 minutes from the MultiPlaza shopping mall and the most modern, best-equipped hospital in all of Central America – Hospital CIMA **(hospitalsanjose.net).** We take an express bus that leaves every 1/2 hour that are quiet, very comfortable, do not allow any standing passengers and the **cost is just over one US dollar**.

How much will this home cost? I have very carefully budgeted US$85K for the completely furnished and equipped home but Scott says to me, "Why don't we just say it's going to be under US$100K."

So yes! You can have a comfortably furnished, two-bedroom, two-bath, 1,200 ft2 house with over 800 ft2 of covered patio for under US$100K.

If you wish, you may consider building a separate apartment or two while building your home. We found it easy to keep our one-bedroom, one-bath apartment rented out in the other house. This added US$325 per month to our income when it was rented and cost us nothing when it was not. Another benefit of the apartment is we have met some very interesting people.

Our thanks to George Lundquist for his contribution. George is the founder of *Costa Rica Retire on Social Security*. George believes that "you measure a man's wealth by the number of things he does NOT need."

Affordable Property Taxes

Taxes should be a major consideration for people moving to Costa Rica to improve their lifestyles. **Income taxes, sales taxes, property transfer taxes** and **property taxes** should be carefully examined. This land is filled with stunning scenery, sunshine and smiles but there are taxes here too.

In the US, the 46,000-page tax code with 481 separate tax forms has become such an absurd and complicated monstrosity that US taxpayers in 2002 spent approximately US$200 billion in the professional preparation of their tax forms - almost 10% of what the IRS actually collects.

Thankfully, Costa Rica taxes are **not quite that complicated.**

When buying a home in Costa Rica, **property taxes and property transfer taxes** must be considered but fortunately there is not much to worry about since Costa Rica **property taxes are only 0.25%** of the recorded property value, which is not always the real market value.

This means that on your US$250,000 luxury, 'getaway' home on the beach, you will owe just US$625 per year in property taxes.

It is important to note that Costa Rica property tax law requires homeowners to file a declaration (*Declaración de Bienes Inmuebles*) with the Municipal government declaring the value of the home every five years.

The **property transfer tax** (*Impuesto de Traspaso*) is 1.5% of the value indicated in the transfer deed or the registered tax value of the property, whichever is higher, and will apply when the title of a property is transferred from the seller to the buyer.

This **can be avoided** when the property is owned in the name of a corporation; then you can buy and sell the corporation which would include the home. **You must be careful, however**, to verify that there are no *surprise* obligations associated with that corporation.

Many Costa Rica homes are on sale for under US$100K, which means that on a US$100K home, you are paying 0.25% which is US$250 per year in property taxes or about US$21 per month.

How does **US$21 per month in property taxes** compare to what you are paying at home?

So What's Where?

Look Around Before Committing

In spite of economic factors that have negatively affected Costa Rica in other ways, the **construction industry is thriving**. The Federated College of Engineers and Architects (*Colegio Federado de Ingenieros y Architectos*, CFIA) estimated that by August 2004 construction was up by 28.41% from the same time last year. Some 950,000m2 of residential housing was built in the first eight months of 2004. That should give you plenty of choice!

Having said that the time is right to invest in property, **there is no need to rush.** There are dozens of gorgeous properties and plots of land around the country so you don't have to bid on the first one you find, however tempting it might seem. You need to **focus on buying the right kind of house,** in the right place at the right price. This takes time, research, patience and foot-slogging.

Don't count on being able to get a mortgage in Costa Rica! It often depends on your legal status. If you are a legal resident of Costa Rica, it's *do-able*, but if not, it may be difficult.

Your ideal home may be perched on a remote ridge with views of mountains and the coast. But you must always **balance your dream with the real value** of a place. That isolated ridge will mean higher construction costs if your materials have to be trucked in from miles away and then up an unpaved track to reach the site, and municipal services may never reach you. Your property should ideally be an investment too, otherwise your dream may become an unmarketable nightmare.

Now, where you want to settle is a whole other contour line on the mountain. As you have read, Costa Rica goes from chilly 2,500-meter (8,200-feet) mountain villages to the *eternal springtime* of the Central Valley towns, down to the heat and humidity of its two coastal regions.

Don't follow the steps of some gringos who rushed to buy their beachfront dream home with sunsets to order and a chorus of howler monkeys in back, only to be bored out of their minds a year later, suffering from the heat, missing like-minded neighbors, drinking themselves into oblivion and unable to sell because as a real estate investment their *dream home* is a dud!

San José And Central Valley

The **majority of expatriates settle in or around the Central Valley**. This is made up of the capital, San José, with satellite cities of Cartago to the east, Alajuela, Heredia, Grecia and Atenas to the north and west. The climate has two basic seasons: dry and wet, but the temperatures stay almost constant between 20°C (68°F) for the mountains to 30°C 86°F) or more once you drop down from San José towards the coast.

Within San José's metropolitan area, the western suburb of Escazú is beginning to lose its pole position as the **gringos' favorite place** to live and play for less crowded, better value neighborhoods. Nearby, you can find warmer climates in the farming towns of Ciudad Colón, Santa Ana and Puriscal (Did you just read George Lunquist's **Affordable Homes in Costa Rica**?) while Cariari near the airport and back towards town to Rohrmoser are highly popular areas.

If you live in Costa Rica, you may be pleased to know that **there is no income tax in Costa Rica** on money earned outside of Costa Rica by legal residents. Even if you earn money in Costa Rica, the personal income taxes are low compared to North America, with many personal expenses deductible from locally earned income. Corporate taxes are also low.

These areas are becoming more developed with the overload from Escazú moving out, but land and houses of both American or more rustic *Tico* design are still available at good prices. The brokers here call this area the "Golden Triangle" and we will look at their prices further on.

In the Central Valley, you are close to all amenities, malls are sprouting like mushrooms, good international schools and clinics are just minutes away and you can still buy a fabulous house with gardens, pool and mountain views for less than back home. Over east, the old capital town of Cartago has very reasonably priced properties, the infrastructure is all there but it has a decidedly although undeserved unfashionable image.

If you work in San José, a daily commute from Cartago can be tiresome even with the (often clogged) two-lane *autopista* that covers most of the 20-km (12.4-mile) drive between the two cities and it is a major trek to get to the airport – a real pain, if you need to travel out of country frequently.

Many gringos have settled in other outlying communities to the north of San José near to Turrialba and around Trés Rios. You will be right out there in all that dramatic countryside and well above the 1000-meter (3,280-feet) line and if that is what you want, there are some fine properties and land plots around.

A best-kept secret with definite bargain opportunities is Heredia, north of San José on the slopes of Barva volcano. It has seen the biggest growth in construction with 49% increase as compared to 14% in 2003.

This self-contained university city now has all the commercial and social infrastructure nearby so you don't need to go into San José although downtown is only 30 minutes away. It also lies close enough to the airport to be convenient without being in the flight path.

The rapid expansion of Heredia is mostly due to commercial and industrial development and it has caused an increase in the per-meter cost of construction. A two-to-three-bedroom house with standard finish (between basic and luxury) will cost about ¢130,000 (US$292) per square meter.

If you want **cool mountain air** and views with positive investment possibilities this is an area to consider.

Outside the Golden Triangle, you can look at areas around the coffee towns like La Garita, Grecia and Atenas in the western Central Valley with their spring-like climates and rural tranquility. Also, they are ideal for accessing the western beaches because they are located close to the main highways that head down to the Pacific.

You are nearly always better off buying the cheapest house in a better neighborhood than the highest priced house in a poor neighborhood. You'll have a much higher probability of making money with the first kind of property.

Escazú – Too Popular?

Escazú, although officially a separate city from San José has been absorbed by the general urban expansion west from the city center.

Made up of three districts: San Miguel, San Rafael and San Antonio, its 35 km2 are home to some 53,000 people. Residential construction is estimated at having increased by 30% since 2000 when nearly 15,000 homes were spread among the three districts.

Escazú is a former farming town that has become a hub of malls, factory outlet stores, fast food joints, night spots and designer boutiques.

High-rise condos have replaced the adobe farmsteads and style is definitely geared to American tastes. Although it enjoys the pick of amenities, schools, restaurants and mountain-view homes, services are beyond saturation point with frequent power outages and water shortages and the narrow roads are almost permanently bottle-necked. If you want genuine *Tiquicia* (feel of Costa Rica), then this might not be the best area for you!

Land prices here are some of the highest in the Central Valley but just to pick out some zones within Escazú, you can see that even within this densely populated district, prices vary tremendously.

Price ranges for land per m2:

Area	$	$
Trejos Montealegre residential	140	180
Trejos Montealegre commercial	150	250
Bello Horizonte	80	150
Golden Mile – Area of Escazú near MacDonalds	350	700
Near Country Club	130	200
Near Country Day International school	50	115
San Antonio, up in hills	30	50

Construction costs vary from US$500 - 600 m2 ($46 – 56 ft2) for low to medium quality to over US$750 (US70 ft2) for luxury finished houses.

In the vast majority of cases, it is **more advantageous to own your home** in the name of a corporation. The corporation will cost well under US$1,000 to buy. Owning your home in this way can save you a lot of headaches and will certainly keep your financial life more private and secure.

Other Regions

At the end of this section, we will look more closely at some of the following regions mentioned below. Costa Rica is as varied as it is beautiful, each area offering something unique that can only be appreciated by visiting each in turn. The differences may be positive: wonderful views with good infrastructure, or less than perfect: poorly maintained roads, prone to flooding, far from an international school. ***How To Buy Costa Rica Real Estate Without Losing Your Camisa*** helps you weigh your options.

Further afield, you may wish to consider windy Lake Arenal with spectacular views of the imposing active Arenal volcano located about three hours away from San José. There are small village communities and a number of Germans and other foreigners have settled in this area and opened businesses related to the tourist industry, especially horseback riding, hiking and wind surfing.

Monteverde, nestled in the hills south of Arenal, started out as a Quaker settlement back in the 1950s and is now a bustling mountain community famed as much for its cultural activities as its renowned reserves, wildlife and sporting activities.

With its notoriously potholed road access (kept that way purposely by residents to avoid mass invasions of vehicles into the villages), it has a Shangri-La feel. Isolated but cultured, simple but beautiful and a very close-knit community, it has become a Mecca for most tourists doing a round-country trip of Costa Rica.

Down south-east, the port town of Golfito has an active, if small, foreign resident community and the main duty-free shopping zone created to offset the moribund banana industry is just outside town. It is also close to the Panama border and the surfer paradise of Pavones.

If you really want remote, look at the Osa Peninsula. The area, which is mostly National Park, is being gradually developed with improved roads and services.

While some bemoan its loss of pristine isolation, it is becoming popular with some gringo and national entrepreneurs opening boutique hotels, dive operations and sports fishing businesses and other enterprises catering to eco-tourists.

Before getting overly enthusiastic about these areas of Costa Rica, read about **Life On The Beach** and concession properties. Different rules apply to beachfront properties but this has not stopped many North Americans and Europeans from buying beachfront homes and many new hotel and vacation apartment developments are planned.

The steady **rise in property values** along the central Pacific coast around Jacó and Manuel Antonio looks set for the time being, especially if the road from San José via Orotina is finally restructured and improved. The beaches here are the closest to San José and demand for homes and holiday properties is high.

Condominium projects in Manuel Antonio, Jacó and (the mid-Pacific as opposed to the north in Guanacaste) Playa Hermosa are selling well. Las Vistas Condominium near Jacó, for example, is offering pre-sales two-bedroom units for US$200K with construction only just starting at the end of 2004. Land prices can fetch between US$25 - 150 m2 (US$2.3 – 14 ft2) depending on how close to the *desirable* areas you are looking!

Serious, **violent crime involving foreigners is rare in Costa Rica** but petty crime which is often easily avoided is quite common. We must not forget that millions of people in Costa Rica make no more than a couple of hundred dollars per month, so if you're driving around in a new car that would cost them the equivalent of ten years gross income – they will think you're a 'rich gringo' and they would be right!

Liberia, located on the Pan-American highway up in Guanacaste province is not only a literal hotspot, but since the upgrading of the airport to full international status, a lot of commercial and residential development is taking place in and around the town.

Without the cooling coastal breezes, this is a hot place and it turns into a virtual dust bowl during the dry season, but it is booming and if property investment is on your list, then take a look around here.

Real estate development in some regions of Costa Rica has taken off and with improved infrastructure, they will boom. Based on comprehensive questionnaires sent to area real estate experts, the following regions of Costa Rica will be more closely examined:

- Atenas and San Ramón, Puntarenas to Parrita
- The southern Caribbean
- The Pacific coastal areas – General overview
- Guanacaste & northwest Pacific
- Nicoya
- Southern Pacific
- The Central Valley

Atenas, San Ramón And Puntarenas To Parrita

Our thanks to Terry Mills of Costa Rica Land & Property for her professional information and knowledge of the Atenas area and mid-Pacific. If you would like more detailed information about real estate in this area, please visit **www.WeLoveCostaRica.com** and then click on **'Help-U-Search'**.

Atenas is said to have the perfect climate with warm days, cool nights and enough rain year round to keep most plant life green and lush. San Ramón is around the 1800m mark making for cooler days often with afternoon mist and definitely chilly nights. Puntarenas, sheltered within the Gulf of Nicoya can be very hot and humid with stifling nights although fresh breezes reach the more southerly areas around Parrita.

Atenas, San Ramón and Puntarenas all have banks, good shopping, medical services (there is a large *Caja* hospital in Puntarenas although most gringos come up to San José for medical and dental care), internet cafés and some restaurants.

About 85% of properties in this area are raw land plots and better value can be found by building your own home than trying to buy ready-made. The area has some great views such as a 28-hectare farm just outside Atenas that has views right down to the Gulf of Nicoya.

You can bring your dog or cat into Costa Rica but you must obtain a Certificate of Good Health issued by your own veterinarian and follow the proper procedure. This must be faxed to the Ministry of Health in Costa Rica. When approved, they will fax you the authorization for the animal to travel to Costa Rica. I would strongly recommend that you work with a Costa Rican veterinarian and arrange everything for your beloved pets long before you book your flights.

Foreign property owners in the region are about 10 – 15% Americans around Atenas with some Germans, Canadians and Colombians but around 40% of beach properties have mixed-nationality foreign ownership.

Security depends on the area but generally an alarm system coupled with a caretaker when you are away is enough. It's best to see whether the neighbors use bars and do the same so as not to be targeted, especially once it is known that the house belongs to a foreigner since that means *wealthy* to most of the criminal sector.

There is **huge, virtually untapped investment potential** in Atenas and surrounding area for recuperation hotels. Costa Rica has a large retirement population with many foreigners coming here to take advantage of cheap cosmetic or other surgery and they would pay well for special-care accommodation while they recover.

This is primarily an agricultural region with no mega-resort development. Instead, there is a lovely 11-room inn located outside Atenas, in a coffee plantation with gorgeous views of the volcanoes and a free-form pool with BBQ area, open-air terraces for dining, nature trails to rivers and waterfalls.

Property prices here depend on many factors such as view, proximity to the ocean, access and services.

Land prices average out as follows: over 100 hectares - US$0.50 - 1 m2 ($0.05 – 0.09 ft2)

Non-beach property that may or may not have great views, can fetch between US$4,900 - 9,800 hectare ($1,984 – 3,967 acre).

As the size goes down the price tends to go up. A plot of land from 1,000 m2 (10,760 ft2) up to 20,000 m2 (215,200 ft2) with a great view, near the ocean (within a half hour or so), good access roads, with electricity and telephone service nearby will start at US$10 m2 ($0.9 ft2) and may go up to US$15 – 20 ($1.4 – 1.86 ft2).

Costa Ricans greet each other by touching their right cheeks and kissing. They don't always actually *kiss* one another; it may just be an 'air kiss.' If you are not a *Tico* then you are not always expected to do this but you may as well get the hang of the local customs.

Beachfront property starts at around US$25 m2 ($2.32 ft2) and may go to US$150 ($14 ft2) or more.

Property in Orotina can run at US$10 m2 ($0.93 ft2) and we have seen a 28-hectare (70 acres) farm north of Puntarenas selling for around US$0.55 m2 ($0.05 ft2). It has a stunning view of the surrounding mountains and even the ocean from the hill top at the center of the farm. Asking prices vary around 10% - 15% over the seller's expectations but one should keep in mind that the asking price for foreigners is often a lot higher. Patience and a good broker are invaluable in getting the best price.

Buyers should **be careful of real estate companies bumping up the price** of property from 10 to a whopping 100% but claiming to charge the buyer only 5%. At Costa Rica Land & Property, we charge a straight 10% to the buyer.

Other scams to watch out for are the mis-use of copied survey plans that are openly available to anyone from the *Registro Nacional* (National Land Registry). Con men will try to sell a property that is not theirs, and lying about boundaries to make them seem bigger is not uncommon. I once heard of someone losing his farm because he bought a *second-hand* corporation instead of transferring title to his own corporation. The trick was that the sellers invented a bill of exchange (*letra de cambio*) predating the sale, stating the corporation owed them money and reclaimed the land in payment.

Value-for-money real estate can be found in the hills around Parrita, Orotina, Atenas and San Ramón especially large lots that can be subdivided and sold off in smaller lots. More often than not, they have ocean views but lack some infrastructure. However, new roads with other services are being rapidly installed and once complete, prices will soar.

When you look at the **stability and security** of real estate investments in Costa Rica, you can understand why prices are rising. That does not include the priceless things so many people take for granted here: the truly friendly character of the people, the best climate in the world and the relaxed pace of things.

Interested in owning a Costa Rica B&B? At **WeLoveCostaRica.com** you will find a Power Point presentation in the Downloads section which will give you some useful information if you are interested in starting your own Costa Rica B&B.

Good private schools are found in Atenas and San Ramón but no fully bilingual international schools. A new mall has just opened in San Ramón and Heredia's new *Paseo de las Flores* mall is only minutes away from Atenas.

The drive from Atenas to the international airport is 20 minutes and from Puntarenas, if the road is clear, one and a half hours.

The main problems in the area from Atenas to Orotina are bad roads, lack of phone lines as well as the usual headaches obtaining concessions and permits for beachfront properties. This is changing with fiber-optic lines and cable internet being installed. Atenas loses water pressure fairly frequently so many houses have water tanks and sweet water can be a problem on the coast. Palo Seco, near to Parrita on the mid-Pacific coast, for example has wells that are contaminated with salt water – the water in this area is all right for washing but not drinking.

But these are compensated by a **wonderful spring-like climate** and an ideal position between the services of San José and access to the beaches. Crime is lower in the hill districts although the more touristy beach areas tend to attract the criminal element.

Squatters are not a common problem in this area being usually attracted to large tracts of land left unattended for long periods of time.

There can be a few problems with title as anywhere else, occasionally originating from family feuds and the beach areas where some municipal authorities have no regulatory plan in force with regard to beachfront concessions. Some people still continue to buy and sell property as if it had title but that means changes to existing structures on the land may not be permitted, and new construction will not be allowed. I have seen existing houses torn down by the municipality.

Very few gated communities are found in Atenas and San Ramón with more in the beach areas, but the majority of the housing is free-standing without a swimming pool. The climate may be too cool in San Ramón for a swimming pool.

There are no mega developments and these would not be appropriate to the area, especially around Atenas, although a new hotel has been built on the Palo Seco beach and a developer is hoping to put in a resort/amusement park in the Jacó area.

The Caribbean Connection

Our thanks to Manuel Pinto of CaribSur Brokers for the following expert information on the Caribbean. If you would like more detailed information about real estate in this area, please visit **WeLoveCostaRica.com** and then click on **'Help-U-Search'**.

In many ways, **the Caribbean side of Costa Rica stands apart** from the rest of the country. For many years, this area was virtually isolated – a situation that went two ways. Many *Ticos* believe the Caribbean is not safe, with a deep-rooted distrust of the Afro-Caribbean settlers, and the *Caribeños* developed a strong identity very different from the rest of the country.

In some respects, it was a lawless, independent region reflecting much more the ebullient, sometimes violent nature of its West Indian heritage. On the other hand, the **Caribbean has a character** and vibrancy found nowhere else in the country.

The inland lowlands are home to a few pioneering ex-pat residents who don't mind the more prolonged rainfall and humidity. The towns along the main San José – Limón highway of Guápiles, Guácimo and Siquirres are bustling agricultural centers and provide most shops and basic services, but the nearest international schools and best medical services are back up the hill in San José, and the Braulio Carillo highway connecting San José to the Caribbean is always victim to blockages from landslides during the frequent heavy rains. However, as witnessed by the January 2005 floods that severely affected much of the Caribbean lowlands, re-opening the highway was top priority to access Limón and acted as the main lifeline for emergency supplies and disaster relief. There is also a twisting back route from Siquirres via Turrialba to Cartago and San José.

The area further south from Limón to Cahuita and Puerto Viejo is struggling to shed its poor man's image as well as its reputation for being rough, tough and unsafe.

However, local hoteliers, tourist operators and residents, fed up with the lack of government support, got together to clean up their towns and re-equip police stations providing better security services to improve the region's reputation. Although drug use and petty thieving prevail, major crime is rare.

What attorneys should you use to buy your home in Costa Rica? You can learn more by reading our articles at **WeLoveCostaRica.com**

Many of the people speak English (kind of!), the beaches are just as spectacular as the Pacific and the cuisine can be delectable.

The southern Caribbean's climate is decidedly different from the rest of the country. It can rain at any time although July and August are known for the heaviest rainfall and September and October can be the most reliable months for clear, dry weather. Further north from Limón to Tortuguero, rainfall is greater with no specific dry season. This does mean that **the Caribbean coast is always green** and the rain forests live up to their name.

Although **hurricanes are extremely rare**, the region can feel the effects with extra offshore heavy rains and winds during hurricane season. On average, temperatures are lower than on the Pacific coast and air conditioning is not necessary. It has a **wonderful variety of beaches** from black, white or golden sand to coral, with deep bays and reefs offshore.

The only CCCBR-affiliated (Costa Rica Chamber of Real Estate Brokers) brokers based on the Caribbean coast, CaribSur Brokers cover the area south from Limón down to Manzanillo. Beachfront land goes from US$30 - 60 m2 ($2.79 ft2) and ocean-view constructions from US$100K - 300K although the market is limited for this kind of property. Inland from the beach, land prices vary from US$5 – $10 m2 ($0.46 – 0.93 ft2) and well inland, about 3 km 1.86 miles) from the beach   for US$0.50 to $4 m2 ($0.046 – 0.37 ft2). Houses in Limón sell for between US$45K - US$200K.

Costa Rica is famous for 'paper developments'. Fancy Websites with dramatic project names, an artist's interpretation of what your home will look like "when it's finished." There's usually lots of *fluff* with a photograph of a massive, ornate entrance to your 'dream' project but unfortunately, too often that ornate entrance is all that ever gets built.

Value-for-money properties are in oceanview homes due to the scarcity of this kind of land although actual beachfront is risky. The local council has no proper zoning plan and almost half the beachfront is protected land in the Gandoca-Manzanillo Wildlife Refuge. **Good investment returns** can be had by buying empty plots to put in quality residential units.

You should expect two to five times the return on property bought in five to ten years, especially with undeveloped land. Costa Rica in general is **increasingly attractive to foreigners** and with internet, non-retirees can still work in remote locations like the southern Caribbean.

As an **antidote to the stress** and insecurity of so many other countries, Costa Rica is a magnet for many foreigners. And for Europeans the Euro against US dollar rates mean investment comes in almost 30% cheaper!

Local feeling is against the huge resort-style tourist complexes sprouting on the Pacific side. Locals will tell you they don't want the high-rise condos or mega-resorts like those being developed over in Guanacaste. The few large resorts such as Hotel Suerre and Las Palmas do not attract much international business and upset locals by abusing environmental guidelines during construction.

Most tourist investment has been into boutique hotels, mid-range B&Bs and surfer hostels. Limón is the nearest airport serviced by local charter planes and scheduled flights by the two domestic lines, SANSA and Nature Air; Juan Santamaría international airport is three and a half to four hours away by road.

Only two small gated communities exist and the majority of homes are single-home properties, mostly standard quality without swimming pools. If worried about security, some home owners employ a full-time caretaker on the property, which is also convenient for general maintenance.

Alarms or even bars on the windows are uncommon. Cahuita has remained a relative backwater for development whereas Puerto Viejo and land down to Manzanillo is booming. Around 60% of land is titled apart from the *Zona Maritimo* lands; squatters are a rare problem as are land title disputes. A title company should not be necessary. Infrastructure is improving with mains water arriving into Punta Uva, south of Puerto Viejo, and full sewage treatment in Manzanillo.

The roads remain a pothole disaster area but it helps keep the slow pace of life as bicycles and pedestrians use the single main road for lack of sidewalks. High-speed internet is reaching the towns with ADSL promised for the whole region in the next months, although you must live within 3 km (1.86 miles) of the main road to receive the DSL signal.

Unlike the Common Law system in the US, the interpretation and application of Civil Law or Napoleonic Law is much more restricted and there is far less interpretation of the law available to judges.

During heavy rains, the road to San José can be cut and low-lying areas flood. The January 2005 floods devastated the region with some 8,500 people forced into temporary shelters although the areas immediately adjoining the main coast road were less affected and the San José to Limón highway was re-opened after a couple of days. Currently, the only banks covering the southern Caribbean are in Bribri, halfway between Puerto Viejo and Cahuita and a *Banco de Costa Rica* branch in Puerto Viejo, which also has its own post office. Otherwise Limón is well represented by the main banks.

A cosmopolitan mix of foreigners have chosen the Caribbean; it is popular with Europeans, west-coast Americans and Canadians. *Ticos* are finally shedding their 'fear' of the Caribbean and are starting to buy property for weekend homes. There's no doubt **the area is lively with parties** most nights in Puerto Viejo; a warning to anyone who values the quiet life. Rental homes are scarce too and could be an investment option to build houses for rent on smaller easy-maintenance plots.

Broker commissions are normally 5% of the final sales price but be careful of real estate companies loading on a huge extra commission without the seller's knowledge or approval. Scotia Bank will offer 8% towards a mortgage but most transactions are paid in full without a mortgage. As anywhere else in the country, **don't think of putting your money down without carefully inspecting the property** and checking for liens.

In this low-lying area, **check out drainage** when much land becomes swampy. Earthquakes do happen so check for cracks in walls or damage to roofing materials. Having said that, full cover home insurance including natural disasters is well worth it.

With increased cruise ship traffic into Limón, business opportunities catering to passengers during their day visits abound. Luxury boutique hotels are needed.

The main medical clinic servicing the area is well placed half-way between Limón and Manzanillo, at Hone Creek, and the state-provided health care is good. However, in keeping with the laid-back, rather hippy image, alternative health care is well represented. If you don't speak Spanish, then don't worry, Caribbean English is spoken by almost everyone.

Are you a Canadian? Are you interested in knowing more about making your tax status *bullet-proof* – At **WeLoveCostaRica.com** you will find this report by a Canadian attorney in the Downloads section.

Some Tips for the Caribbean

1. **Speak to neighbors** about the property that interests you to see if there are any *unofficial* issues.
2. **Check the land and drainage** during the wet season. Does it have water in the dry season? Does it flood in the rainy season?
3. Re-learn the meaning of the word 'patience'.
4. **Spend time in the country** and the town of your choice before making the final decision.
5. In small towns such as these, **never believe** the word on the street; rumors get grotesquely distorted whenever news happens!
6. Buy under a corporation to avoid personal liability.

Pacific Coastal Areas – A General Overview

Some areas are booming so fast it's like watching fireworks. To most of us, the beach is special - there is something about living near to the ocean that has people daydreaming about at least a weekend home within the sound of the surf and the shade of palm fronds. However, buying on the beach has its own very specific conditions and legal regulations in Costa Rica.

Guanacaste and the northern Pacific beaches have been earmarked by heavy-investment foreign resort developers; millions of dollars are being poured into the area and luxury, exclusive communities and resorts are emerging for high-flying celebrity clients. Some of the quaint fishing towns have become bustling tourist centers with little character left and conflicts have emerged with resident populations competing with giant developers for precious water resources and land access rights.

Tamarindo, Flamingo and Papagayo are three places in question; they are the closest beach towns to the newly reconditioned, international airport in Liberia and have attracted the heftiest outside investment.

Apart from enjoying the **sunniest, driest climate** in the whole country, Guanacaste benefited from the opening of Liberia's Daniel Oduber airport to full international air traffic in December, 2002 instead of just special charter flights. This has brought about a steep rise in tourists and potential full-time investors.

Delta, Continental and American Airlines are now operating out of the airport, which has seen an 800% increase in commercial flights in the past two years with a **90% increase in tourists** compared to the previous year!

> **Do not automatically trust someone** just because they are fellow countrymen. There have been numerous American, Canadian and sometimes European scam artists operating throughout Mexico, Central America and here in Costa Rica.

The knock-on effect of improved accessibility is reflected in increased demand for property as visitors come into the area, attracted by the ease of getting there, and more brokers are lying in wait only too ready to do business.

The increasing influx of tourists to the northwest Pacific (and other Costa Rica destinations too) is conditioned by likely hotel room shortages. According to the National Chamber of Tourism and the Association of Tourism Professionals, the increase in tourists arriving by air to Liberia has averaged 8.26 percent in the last seven years, while the number of new hotel rooms has averaged only 3.26 percent. Buying into property with a view to exploiting this market **could bring some high-profit returns** even though initial outlay will be greater than in other parts of the country.

The Minister of Tourism, Rodrigo Castro, explained in October 2004 that he has been meeting with both local and international investors to promote new construction and expand existing facilities, to keep up with demand.

Up to now, most tourist development has been small-scale, boutique hotels and single-owner B&Bs. Nonetheless, major resort development is taking off with the Peninsula Papagayo Project, Hacienda Pinilla and Conchal Resort developments, detailed below.

As a result, residential property prices near Papagayo and Playa Hermosa are climbing sharply but there are good investment opportunities to be found along the many beaches and bays that garland this northern coast down to the Nicoya peninsula.

As demand outstrips supply, anyone who gets in on this market opportunity should be **sitting on a healthy investment**. Currently, condos around Flamingo and Playa Potrero are effectively sold out so it's a matter of waiting for the new constructions to take place.

Ocean view condominiums are being planned and built in Playa del Coco, Playa Hermosa and Playa Panamá. Even down to the southern tip of the Nicoya Peninsula from Nosara to Malpaís, prices are beginning to climb as demand rises sharply.

What healthcare options are available in Costa Rica for **veterans?** You can learn more by reading our articles at **WeLoveCostaRica.com**

'Value' and 'price' are not always the same when it comes to Costa Rica real estate. You can learn more by reading our articles at **WeLoveCostaRica.com.**

Looking for the latest Costa Rica news headlines in English? Every week in the News section of **WeLoveCostaRica.com** you will find the latest news headlines. Our thanks to our friends at *La Nación*, which is Costa Rica's most influential and largest Spanish-circulation newspaper. for their permission to include their weekly news reviews.

Want to see how a US businessman runs a successful multi-million-dollar business in the US while enjoying life in Costa Rica? You can learn more by reading our articles at **WeLoveCostaRica.com**

Prices around Flamingo and Playa Hermosa for two-bedroom luxury condos with full management services, sports facilities, restaurants and security go between US$200K to US$450K.

Guanacaste – Beaches Lined With Gold

Scott MacDougall of Century 21 At The Beach provides this expert information on Guanacaste. He has lived and worked in Costa Rica for the last 12 years, specifically involved in real estate, construction and land development. He also spent five years as the Director of Marketing and Sales for the largest and most successful gated resort community in Costa Rica. If you would like more detailed information about real estate in this area, please visit **WeLoveCostaRica.com** and then click on **'Help-U-Search'**.

The northwest coast of Costa Rica is one of the fastest-growing and **hottest real estate markets** in all of Costa Rica. Approximately 95% of all coastal real estate property being purchased in Costa Rica is going to Americans. The remaining 5% is a mix of Canadian, European and South-American purchasers.

The primary reason for this incredible growth over the last 24 months very simply is **ease of access.** Combine that with its enviably sunny and dry climate and the special government approval conceded to the Papagayo Project and this region seems to be a win-win for real estate investors.

Access is the key ingredient to the popularity and within a 13-month period, the revamped Liberia international airport went from having no US commercial airline traffic at all, to having 18 direct US commercial airline flights

Presently Liberia receives direct flights from the major carriers Delta Airlines, Continental Airlines and American Airlines with all three carriers providing direct flights from their major hubs Atlanta, Houston and Miami, respectively. Just over 90,000 passengers landed in Liberia in 2004. Projections for 2005 have over 180,000 passengers arriving at the Liberia airport.

Costa Rica is now only two and a half hours away from these major hubs.

When you are about to enter someone's home in Costa Rica, even if you know the people well, the courteous and respectful tradition requires you to ask, "*Con permiso*" which means, "With your permission?" *before* you actually enter. They will then say, "*Adelante*" or, "*Pase*" which means, "Come on in".

Property prices have definitely changed over the last two years and especially over the last year. We believe they will continue to rise over the next few years as the Liberia international airport receives flights from new routes as well as having existing routes increase their passenger arrivals. As a result **demand for coastal real estate will increase** and prices will increase accordingly.

Similar to other developing and active real estate markets, prices in the northwestern Pacific market area are very much related to infrastructure and distance from the airport. Infrastructure being defined as paved roads, public water system, available electricity, telephone service and a service center (town).

Prices are much higher in areas that can provide the above and are within a 60-90-minute drive to and from the airport. The table below estimates various prices along the northwest Pacific coast.

LOCATION	DRIVE TIME FROM AIRPORT	DISTANCE FROM SERVICE CENTER	ACCESS VIA PAVED ROADS	OCEAN VIEW PROPERTY US$ xM2	BEACH FRONT PROPERTY US$ x M2	BEACH FRONT PROPERTY US$ X FT2
Playa Hermosa	25 mins	8 kms	Yes	US$80 - US$150	US$250 - US$300	US$23.2 US$27.8
Playas del Coco	25 mins	0 kms	Yes	US$60 - US$100	US$150 - US$200	US$14 US$18.5
Flamingo	65 mins	0 kms	Yes	US$ 65 - US$125	US$200 - US$250	US$18.5 US$23.2
Tamarindo	70 mins	0 kms	Yes	US$100 - US$200	US$350 - US$450	US$35.2 US$41.8
Nosara	2 hours & 15 mins	32 kms	No	US$50 - US$100	US$75 - US$125	US$7 US$11.6
Samara	2 hours	0 kms	Yes	US$50 - US$100	US$100 - US$150	US$9.3 US$14
Playa Coyote	3 hours	60 kms	No	US$25 - US$50	US$50 - US$100	US$4.6 US$9.3

The above noted prices are averages. Prices do vary relative to the property being in gated communities with some common amenities, or free standing.

The market area within 90 minutes of Liberia airport with decent infrastructure is presently a strong sellers market. As such, listing prices and sales prices are close to being one and the same.

Is moving to Costa Rica the right move for you? You can learn more by reading our articles at **WeLoveCostaRica.com**

Resort Communities

There are three operating resort communities on the northwest Pacific coast. All have the standard facilities and amenities of international resorts. In addition, all three offer home sites, condos, and villas. The sales programs at all three locations have met with great success.

- **Conchal Resort** was the second resort community to open in Costa Rica. This property has a 400-room Meliá Hotel, a beautiful Robert Trent Jones Jr. signature golf course, and they are working on selling out their third phase of condominiums with prices ranging from US$280K to US$650K. The developers have invested over US$120 million into this

2,100-acre property. They have generated property sales of over US$45 million in the last three years.

- **Hacienda Pinilla** is the largest single-development property in Costa Rica with a total land area of just under 6,000 acres. Hacienda Pinilla has a Mike Young golf course, along with a small 20-room boutique hotel. The developer has installed over eight miles of roads, and 20 miles of water and electrical lines. Golf course homes and lots sell from US$65K to over US$1 million.

  They are presently working on a new project that offering a golf course and beachfront luxury town homes. Prices range from US$375K to US$750K. Pinilla has developed a master plan in which they wish to sell specific smaller projects to other developers. The developer of Hacienda Pinilla has invested approximately US$65 million in the project.

- **Peninsula Papagayo Project** offers a Four Seasons Resort Hotel near to Conchal along with a stunning Arnold Palmer signature golf course, which opened in January, 2004. This is the first of a three-phase development being built as part of the Peninsula Papagayo Project luxury destination.

  The next two phases will include two more golf courses, two marinas, additional hotels (rumor has it that Ritz Carlton, The Rosewood Group, and the Aman Group have signed letters of intent for boutique hotel sites in Phases II & III), as well as luxury homes and condominiums. Two- and three-bedroom, 2,400-ft2 villas are on sale for US$2.1 to US$2.8 million. Home sites are selling from US$750K to US$2.2 million. The projected budget for all three phases is just under US$400 million. Thus far, the developers have invested over US$110 million into this 2,000 acre project. Most home owners will build their own pools.

If you find a property that you just love and then discover that there are liens of any kind upon the property, you must be extremely cautious! Legal matters can move very, very slowly in this country. We know people that have been fighting problem real estate cases for more than ten years.

It typically takes a total of 12 months to design, permit and build a home.

The northern Pacific zone is fortunate to have three US-trained home builders. This is an advantage to the client as language is not an issue. There is an immediate understanding of the accepted business practices and the process is structured in such a fashion that both the builder and the client are comfortable.

Property management companies are available to maintain homes, lawns, gardens, pools and pay all bills. This service, for an ocean-view home with a pool on a half-acre lot, costs approximately US$200 per month.

Rumors and warnings about squatters are rampant, but in the 12 years that I have been on the northwest Pacific coast, **I have never known anyone that has had any problems with them.**

Property purchasers can acquire title guaranty for their property if they wish. The cost ranges from 0.5% to 1.0% of the purchase price. These same companies will offer escrow accounts and escrow services during the purchase process.

Although there is a fair amount of petty theft in Costa Rica, luckily, there is **very little violent crime,** and in our specific area, Playa Hermosa, there is very little crime of any kind. We are more of a residential community and as such do not attract the same people and criminal elements that haunt more commercialized beach communities.

Some home owners put bars on their windows but the majority of home sites being sold are in gated communities and the owners choose not to install bars on their windows. Many of the new homes have alarm systems.

Whatever you do in Costa Rica with banking, applying for residency or driver's license, **always take photocopies of all documents**. It is not advisable to allow anyone to take your important original documents unless you have photocopies.

Over the last ten years in this area, **property values have appreciated by at least 750%**. In the last two years, on average, property values have doubled. With the doubling of passengers coming into Liberia in 2005, the opening up of new and additional routes into the airport and the effects of the Baby Boomers, we do not see the increase in property values slowing down.

We have advised all our long-term clients that this is a definite acquisition period, no matter if the purchase is oceanview, flat, a home, condo or villa. They should all appreciate and appreciate well. A conservative estimate or minimum would be a rate of 15% for the next year.

The factors that make the northwest Pacific more attractive than other coastal areas are:
- **proximity** to the Liberia international airport (25-minute drive) and the closest beach communities to the airport;

- **better-than-average infrastructure** (roads, water, telephone service);

- immediate service town (five-minute drive) with bank, full-size grocery store, pharmacy, post office, doctor, dentist, official port of entry, hardware stores, computer shop;

- a large service town, Liberia, Guanacaste Province's capital (30-minute drive), a town of 35,000 people;

- **more sun hours** and a drier climate than any other area in Costa Rica;

- the **Four Seasons Resort** and Arnold Palmer golf course, this being the first phase of a major three-phase development;

- a public **golf course**, 50% completed and a 20-minute drive away;

- **wonderful ocean views** with many bays facing west for spectacular sunset views.

- Playa Hermosa, a beautiful one-mile beach that is a **perfectly safe for swimming** and cleaned daily. It is a Blue Flag beach, Costa Rica's top environmental designation;

- **medical clinics** within a 10-minutes drive as well as a major hospital 30 minutes away. A permanent trauma ambulance is stationed ten minutes away;

- a very strong and progressive Residents' Association exists with a well-established expatriate community;

- four bilingual private schools in Liberia and an international school near Tamarindo;

- high-speed internet service to be installed in the first quarter of 2005.

If you plan on buying property solely for investment purposes and do not plan on living in it, to avoid any potential squatter problems, you can normally hire a reliable caretaker for less than US$100 per week. Pay the minimum wage and social security benefits and always get signed receipts as proof of payment. Make sure your property's boundaries are obvious, well fenced and post signs clearly showing the owner's name and contact information.

Nicoya – Bargains Can Still Be Found.

The Nicoya Peninsula in the Central Pacific is still a relatively undeveloped area and **land prices are lower** than the Guanacaste hotspots around Tamarindo or Papagayo described above. Since the opening of the Tempisque bridge, access is faster, although it is still possible to take the Puntarenas ferry to Playa Naranjo or, if you want to protect your car, Paquera, since the still-unpaved 40-km (24.8-mile) stretch south from Naranjo is a killer to any suspension.

The climate at the southern tip of the Peninsula has more rainfall throughout the year and temperatures range from 22°C (71.6° F) during the rainy season or winter, to the high 30s in the dry season or summer.

Infrastructure is adequate but unsophisticated with commercial outlets and medical facilities in Cóbano for the Tambor area. Playa Tambor has the only airstrip on the Peninsula (25 minutes to San José on scheduled domestic flights), the main fishing pier and a sprawling beachfront Barceló Resort with Los Delfines Golf & Country Club, also Barceló-controlled, next door.

There are some very *strange* home designs in Costa Rica and even though you may fall in love with one, you should remember that these houses are typically the most difficult to sell.

Partly as a knock-on effect from the boom further up the coast in Guanacaste, the Nicoya Peninsula is also growing, attracting more tourism and property investors. Bahía Ballena by Playa Tambor has been earmarked for a proposed marina to be built within two years. With the main road paved from the ferry landing in Paquera to Cóbano, the area is more easily accessible with the resulting increase in property values.

A titled beach property on the Peninsula three years ago would have cost you US$100K. Today, that same beachfront lot would cost you US$165K. The southern part of the Peninsula is just starting to boom compared to other beach communities further north, such as Tamarindo and Conchal.

Compare a 1/3-acre titled beachfront lot in Playa Tambor for US$160K to a ¼-acre titled beachfront lot in the Tamarindo area priced at US$450K.

If you would prefer ocean view, a 1¾-acre parcel in Playa Tambor would cost you US$100K compared to ½-acre in Tamarindo priced at US$185K. If you compare the Peninsula to other areas on the Pacific Coast, prices are still affordable, so **buying property in this area is a smart** and secure investment. With more and more American and Canadian buyers arriving, we are seeing a steady growth pattern each year.

If you would prefer to **build your own home** within a residential community, you can purchase two acres with ocean view in the community of Tambor Hills for approximately US$105K. Hotels and B&Bs are for sale, beachfront or ocean view, ranging in price from US$175K up to US$7.8 million.

For rental home options, the Barceló-owned Los Delfines Resort estate offers two-to-three-bedroom villas from US$130K to US$285K with financing, security, maintenance and full resort amenities.

When you decide to buy a new property, **you must be certain** that the property will be yours and that no liens or other impediments will prevent your free use. Obviously, every situation differs but in some cases a review of the Public Registry record will not be enough to uncover all encumbrances. That is why it is important that the buyer have his or her own attorney conduct an independent title search and investigation rather than rely on the seller's attorney.

Southern Pacific Zone

Our thanks to Daveed Hollander of Coldwell Banker Dominical Realty for his expert information on property included in this zone. If you would like more detailed information about real estate in this area, please visit **WeLoveCostaRica.com** and then click on **'Help-U-Search'**.

The climate along the southern Pacific zone is hot and humid on the beach, but things cool down dramatically once you climb into the hills. The mountains fall almost into the ocean in places, so many home-owners can **enjoy a cooler climate** with a gorgeous ocean view thanks to the higher elevations.

In general, the cost of living here, as in the rest of Costa Rica, is much lower than in the US and a family of four should be able to manage comfortably on US$2,000 per month (exclusive of house payments, rent or car).

Many buyers are looking for beach-view lots to build vacation or retirement homes and more buyers are prepared to build rather than buy ready-made. Several multi-million-dollar houses have been built and demand for suitable commercial centers with shops, restaurants and offices is high. Surfing is a big-time activity with two surf schools in Playa Dominical alone.

Steady growth is predicted from Manuel Antonio to the Osa Peninsula, according to Coldwell Banker Dominical Realty. Growth has averaged 15 – 30% over the past few years.

Approximate values for property in the area can be seen as follows:

- Undeveloped beachfront commercial land is the most expensive, averaging US$80K to US$200K per acre (US$197K to US$494K per hectare).

- Residential sites with ocean views and rural acreage cost about US$20K to US$50K per acre (US$49K to US$123K per hectare). Some properties are priced at US$100,000 per acre (US$247K per hectare).

- Large farms and rural land plots run about US$5,000 to US$10K per acre (US$12K to US$25K per hectare).

- Owners should plan on spending US$538 to US$1,076 m2 ($50 – 100 ft2) to build new homes with high-quality construction standards. Already-built luxury homes can run to US$1,345 to US$2,152 m2 $125 – 200 ft2), including the land.

Occasionally the final sales price has exceeded the asking price where multiple bids have occurred. **The best returns** are in all areas: raw land, condos, rentals, hotels and stand-alone homes.

Interested in new homes for under US$100K? We have articles on this very topic at **WeLoveCostaRica.com** with Websites that you can visit and see for yourself.

International developers are showing more interest and prices are rising to compare with other tropical resort areas in the world.

Dominical is a hub town with two mid-size hotels, and several luxury beachfront villa complexes are planned for 2005. It also has adequate shopping amenities. There is an elementary school at nearby Playa Dominical and a high school in Uvita, but the nearest international schools are in San Isidro, Manuel Antonio or in San José.

Manuel Antonio, Quepos, Uvita and Ojochal also have reasonable shopping facilities.

Playa Dominical is about three and a half hours from San José's international airport and airstrips exist for scheduled local flights and charters into Quepos and Palmar Sur.

Medical and banking services are in San Isidro, Quepos, Manuel Antonio and Palmar Sur.

The police force is supported by the local community and although petty crime exists, it is lower than in other areas.

Infrastructure has improved with repaved roads, piped water and cellular telephone coverage. High-speed internet connections are hooked up along the main roads.

Property taxes range from 0.25% for titled properties to 6% for Maritime Zone concessionary properties. Many home-owners pay annual dues to the municipal authority for road maintenance and water services of around US$500 to US$1,000 per year.

If you only want to spend some of the year in the zone, then your best deal is a small house in a gated community or condo. There are some communities that offer timeshare with full management services.

Before buying, **have a full inspection done of the land**, especially for soil stability and water runoffs or flooding.

Moving abroad with a new baby? You can learn more by reading our articles at **WeLoveCostaRica.com**

Home owners in the area use a mix of security systems, going from barking dogs to complex alarm systems, and several employ live-in caretakers.

In summary, our friends at Coldwell Banker Dominical Realty offer these tips for buying real estate: find property with **easy access**, water, utilities, view (preferably ocean view), and excellent location. Investigate title insurance and guarantees, and **retain your own legal counsel** to represent you and review the sales contract.

As you can see, what Costa Rica lacks in square miles, it more than makes up for in variety. But there's only one way for you to appreciate this. You have to be here and explore, choose the climate that suits you best, pick an elevation that appeals, the community that feels right. Consider whether you want city comforts or rural remoteness, the hills or the beach, hot or cool – chances are, you'll find it somewhere in Costa Rica.

Prices for houses vary just as they vary in your home town. If you want to live in a huge mansion in the most expensive area of the country you can spend millions of dollars. If you want to live in a typical middle-class area near San José, you can find numerous properties for under US$150K. If you prefer to live in the country, you can find many properties for under US$100K

Chapter Two

Finding A Real Estate Broker

A good, professional real estate broker can either help you make a good decision to buy into Costa Rica, or you can go home disillusioned about how the property market is managed here and shocked at the ridiculously high asking prices being touted to most North American clients.

Some **excellent Costa Rica real estate professionals** are operating with thick portfolios of happy clients but finding them is the challenge. Understandably, the top brokers are in demand and have so much business they simply don't bother to advertise nor have the time to put up and maintain a Website even though the internet is flooded with dubious real estate sites.

Looking for them on the internet just won't work! This is where *How To Costa Rica Real Estate Without Losing Your Camisa* can help you. We are in touch with the most professional, hard-working, conscientious brokers in the country; those with experience and the know-how to guide you through the real estate process.

Want to see why *The Wall Street Journal* ranked Costa Rica #1 a few years ago? You can learn more by reading our articles at **WeLoveCostaRica.com**

As you have read in the first section of **What's Where,** the real estate industry has been growing rapidly in many parts of Costa Rica over the past ten years and it looks like continuing for at least the next decade. That means all sorts of real estate companies and brokers have appeared on the scene and frankly, **some of them have no idea** what they are doing.

Just as you would back home, you need to find an experienced professional to help with your requirements.

Need to know what to be careful about in building your own home in Costa Rica? You can learn more by reading our articles at **WeLoveCostaRica.com**

Do I Really Need A Real Estate Broker?

No, it is possible to go it alone, and even though we have outlined them earlier in this book, ask yourself these basic questions first:

- **Do you speak fluent Spanish?**

- Do you know how to go about researching a property here?

- What about Costa Rica's **complicated laws** pertaining to owning property here, especially on the beach?

- **Do you understand the system of law** in Costa Rica? The Civil (Napoleonic) Code, which is different from the Common Laws that you may be accustomed to?

- Frankly, do you have the energy, Spanish, contacts and training to do a good job on your own?

These are fundamental issues, making it all the more important to find a reliable broker to help you out. For these reasons alone, **we do recommend that you use a qualified and experienced broker.**

The self-regulating Costa Rica Chamber of Real Estate Brokers (CCCBR) has been functioning since 1974 with a membership of some 220 brokers who cover residential, commercial and industrial real estate. Although they are not subject to any state regulatory controls, members agree to follow an ethical code of professional conduct and are lobbying to enforce mandatory licensing for all brokers.

As they outline in their mission statement, "The broker is not, as some people think, someone who sells property, **but a professional who can properly advise and represent** a client in a real estate transaction".
That sounds fine and dandy but the reality is most brokers want to have the purchaser and the seller reach an agreement as quickly as possible with a nice fat commission for themselves.

A professional, caring broker will advise you on price, financing, contracts, taxes, obligations, transfer fees and terms. He or she should also give you a copy of the registered survey map of the property and its unique registration number (*folio real*) free of charge. Even if you go through the Chamber, however, not every affiliated broker may be right for you.

'Value' and 'price' are not always the same when it comes to Costa Rica real estate. You can learn more by reading our articles at

WeLoveCostaRica.com.

Looking for the latest Costa Rica news headlines in English? Every week in the News section of **WeLoveCostaRica.com** you will find the latest news headlines. Our thanks to our friends at *La Nación*, which is Costa Rica's most influential and largest Spanish-circulation newspaper. for their permission to include their weekly news reviews.

Want to see how a US businessman runs a successful multi-million-dollar business in the US while enjoying life in Costa Rica? You can learn more by reading our articles at **WeLoveCostaRica.com**

House-hunting is a very personal thing - and you have to *click* with your broker.

If you are not happy with the service you get from one, then find another and ask questions to make sure they can give you what you want. The brokers you come across may be local *Ticos* or a gringo just like yourself, but **don't assume** that having someone of your own nationality showing you around is any guarantee of experience and professionalism!

You have already read in **What Major Hurdles Will You Face?** that brokers are not licensed in Costa Rica so anyone can set up to try to sell you property, and many do. They make their money by selling on a commission basis and have no license to forfeit so you are the one that will lose out by choosing the wrong person! Their commissions of 5-10% are paid by the seller giving you an idea of where their loyalties might lie.

Interested in using pre-fabricated materials to build an affordable home in Costa Rica? You can learn more and read out articles at **WeLoveCostaRica.com**

Some Tips (And Awkward Questions To Ask!) When Looking For A Real Estate Broker:

- Does the real estate broker have **any formal training** at all in real estate? Ask **how long they have been in the business** and if possible, try to get a recommendation from a previous client.

- If they are *not* Costa Rican, **is the broker a legal resident** of Costa Rica?

- If non-*Tico*, **does the broker speak good enough Spanish** so that you can trust they understand what's going on in the local markets. (Can you imagine buying real estate from someone in your own country that doesn't speak your language well?)

- If they are *Tico,* **do they speak English well?** Are they helping you to understand the Spanish small print?

- Do they keep **up-to-date listings** of properties for sale or rent?

- Do they work **full time** as a real estate broker?

- How many properties have they sold in the last three months?

- Do they specialize in a specific area of the market?

- How many **listings** do they have?

- Do they **show up on time** for appointments, reply to your emails promptly and return your telephone calls?

- Do they have a **list of references** that you can call?

- Are you convinced that they are going to **look out for your best interest?** Remembering that the sales commission will be paid to them by the seller, they may *care* more about the seller and not you, the buyer.

- Have they truly tried to find out exactly what type of property you want, rather than hauling you around to show off places that are unsuitable and may be selling for much higher prices than you have requested?

- **Beware the 'bait and switch'** brokers who habitually advertise a *once-in-a-lifetime* price on a fantastic property that was never actually for sale to grab your interest and then try to sell you a higher-priced property. Some properties may have sold by the time you arrive to look at them but there are brokers out there who play this game all day long.

There Is A Reason Why Brokers Are As They Are

Before you think that we are dead against brokers operating in Costa Rica, be assured that this is not the case. At the opening of this book, we said that there are some very good professional brokers around. The problem is finding them and that is how we can help you by logging onto **WeLoveCostaRica.com** for information. But you might be wondering why it is that a number of these so-called 'brokers' don't seem to be sincerely representing your interests or needs.

Have no doubts that it can be a pretty desperate business for a broker working with one of the *big-name* real estate companies here, or running a franchise in one of the outlying regions. **No wonder they are interested in bigger commissions**.

To take out a franchise or be able to represent a well-known company, a broker often has to put out quite a lot of money for the privilege.

When someone gives you directions from a specific landmark, confirm that the landmark is still there! I remember one frustrating afternoon trying to find someone in San Jose. His directions said that his offices were 50 meters west of a particular hotel. I tried finding this hotel for about forty minutes. His line was busy but when we eventually spoke on the telephone, he confessed that the hotel was not actually there any more and said "But everyone knows **the hotel used to be** there." Hmmm!

A broker may have to pay:

- transport and accommodation for an obligatory international broker/owner conference;
- a franchise fee for a set time (which could be five years) of up to $20,000;
- a monthly management fee for each broker in the franchise;
- advertising fees to help promote the mother company;
- regional development fees to help promote the region represented by that broker;
- a broker service fee of 1.5% for all successfully closed deals per month;
- annual membership of around $350 per year.

Is it any wonder that some are tempted to push for the high-end deals in the market where commissions are higher? Does it surprise you now that maybe your best interests as a buyer looking for the best deal may not be exactly at the core of a broker's objective of selling high and selling fast?

Chapter Three

Renting

Over and again, you will read or hear the advice to **test the waters** before leaping into the balmy but sometimes murky ocean of full-time life in a different country. This also applies to moving to a different part of your own country.

Costa Rica is no different. Many foreigners are living here and loving the choice they have made to settle down, but it just might not be the place for you and **the best way** to find out without losing too much money is to come visit and rent a place as your base for getting to know the country.

Maybe you aren't into buying at all but still want to live here long-term. You need a place to live and renting is your obvious option.

In most cases, foreigners have the same rights as nationals with regard to property, especially renting, but t what are the ins and outs of renting property in Costa Rica?

The revised Rent Law was introduced in 1995, replacing an older law that gave almost total protection to tenants and making eviction virtually impossible. This led to problems with landlords unable to evict tenants-from-hell, neglected rental properties and lots of bad feeling.

Addresses are *different* here. Unlike the rest of the world that have addresses, zip codes or postal codes, the Costa Ricans don't actually give you *addresses*, they will give you physical directions. My telephone bill lists my address as being 700 O (oeste = west) 100 S (sur = south) 150 O (oeste = west) from a specific landmark. So when you are asked to meet someone at a place you don't know in Costa Rica, try and get really specific directions.

Nowadays, landlords have to give at least three months' notice but at least they can get rid of unscrupulous tenants. As a tenant, you are still in a very strong position and well protected by the law when you sign a rental agreement, as long as you comply with such basic conditions as paying the rent on time!

Looking for the latest Costa Rica news headlines in English? Every week in the News section of **WeLoveCostaRica.com** you will find the latest news headlines. Our thanks to our friends at *La Nación*, which is Costa Rica's most influential and largest Spanish-circulation newspaper. for their permission to include their weekly news reviews.

Want to see how a US businessman runs a successful multi-million-dollar business in the US while enjoying life in Costa Rica? You can learn more by reading our articles at **WeLoveCostaRica.com**

Location And Price

The rental choices are bewildering. Imposing condominiums tower over traditional adobe single-storey homes in Escazú. Office and apartment blocks cluster downtown. Simple *Tica* houses sit cozily within their gardens. Sumptuous mansions nestle in the hills and students crowd into single-room studios with shared kitchen and bath. But your rights are similar in all cases.

The exceptions are fully equipped apart-hotel units offering mid-term deals that don't come under the rent law. These are a good choice to use as a base if you want to come into Costa Rica for a couple of months only.

The other exception is the special law relating to condominiums that have shared maintenance fees and other costs as determined by the General Assembly of Owners (see the section on **Condominiums**).

Many residential rentals are offered furnished, which is not always ideal if you have moved into Costa Rica with all your worldly belongings, and of course, **the landlord's taste will rarely reflect yours**!

It can sometimes be possible to work a deal to have furniture removed and pay less rent but if you agree on keeping the furniture, be very clear about 'wear and tear' on furnished accommodation and have any special conditions stipulated in the tenancy agreement.

Be aware that the currency you use to pay your rent affects your rights. Paying your rent in the local currency, colones, **allows for a 15% annual adjustment** on your rent. However, if you agree to pay in US dollars, the contract is yours for **three years without adjustment**, but once it comes up for renewal, that's when trouble can start if the owner decides to push for a an overly optimistic price hike.

Have a look at the section below, **Rents You Can Expect To Pay and Where**, for some guidelines on what rents are going for.

Avoiding Trouble

So, what if you and your landlord can't agree on the rent increase? If you want to stay on in the property but think that the rent increase is unfair, you have recourse to arbitration initially without hiring a lawyer. Proceedings can be started in the Small Claims Court (*Juzgado de Menor Cuantía*) by one or other party involved registering their disagreement.

The Court, usually working out of the respective town hall for your area, determines what an acceptable rent adjustment should be but it only deals with values of ¢600.000 (US$1,350) or less. For higher amounts, you will have to go to a higher Court (*Tribunal*) and that means contracting legal assistance.

The landlord usually requests that the Court agree to an increase of more than the 15% per year established in colón-based rental contracts and if this is ratified, the tenant must pay that amount to continue renting the property in question.

If the tenant contests the decision, an appraisal expert named from the Court's official list visits the property and calculates its rental worth based on quality and age of construction, current condition, neighborhood and inflation rate.

Once this report is presented, either side can accept or reject its findings. Such is human nature that the landlord usually complains that the estimate is too low and the tenant that it is too high.

Arbitration can continue by appointing lawyers who can demand further justification of the expert's appraisal. As often happens, the only ones to win out are the lawyers! Although stalemate can ensue, the final ruling is usually accepted and landlords adjust their rents accordingly. Don't be shy about negotiating - it's a buyer's market just now and you are in strong position to work things your way.

Remember that in Costa Rica, the size of the terrace and garage will sometimes be included in the 'living area' whereas in the US and Canada that does not tend to be the case. So a 2,000 ft2 home in Costa Rica may only be considered a 1,700 ft2 home in the US.

The Rent Law (*Ley De Inquilinato*) Explained

The law protects both sides pretty evenly but this is what you should know before signing on the dotted line:

- Contracts can be **written or verbal**.

- Contracts are **valid for three years** minimum if all rental conditions are met.

- Contracts **automatically renew** for a further three years unless the landlord gives at least three months notice before the contract expires.

- If the rent is paid in colones, an annual **increment of 15% applies**. Rent adjustments in other currencies only apply when the contract is to be renewed and both parties agree. Rents requested in dollars can be paid in colones at the current rate of exchange.

- Public services and **utilities are paid by the tenant** unless otherwise agreed. Property taxes by the landlord.

- Necessary repairs with due access by workmen must be allowed by the tenant.

- If sold, the property's new owners **must respect** any existing rental contract.

- Any improvements made by a tenant become the landlord's property.

- The use of a property cannot be changed: a residence cannot become a shop.

- Landlords may inspect their property every month.

- Tenants can pay rents up to seven days after the stipulated due date.

- The landlord can ask for a maximum **deposit of guarantee** equivalent to one month's rent.

- Tenants cannot sub-let the property.

Rental prices vary dramatically. Friends of mine have rented a brand new two-bedroom apartment for US$400 per month. We also know people who are renting a huge, luxurious four-bedroom home for US$3,000 per month.

Make sure you understand the contract. If not, have it translated into your language and notarized. It might seem like an unnecessary expense but it could save trouble later on.

Rents You Can Expect To Pay And Where

So what's on offer? With such a wide choice of properties available, it is impossible to give general overviews. And since **there is no real Multiple Listing Service** (MLS), it's even more varied here than in North America.

However, there are two streams of real estate running side by side in Costa Rica: the less luxurious, **typical, *Tico* houses** and the **American-style properties** you are probably familiar with back home. By that, we mean larger family homes or apartments with spacious kitchen-dining areas, big bathrooms, more open-plan room designs and imported fittings. Both cater to different markets, both are found in different ways, both can vary tremendously in price.

The real estate market in some areas is sluggish, so remember that in these areas, you, the buyer, are in control. If you have any doubts about an area, why not suggest to the seller that you live in and rent the home that you are considering buying for six months first? Negotiate a deal so that when you are finally sure you want to buy, a percentage of your rent paid is credited towards the purchase price?

Tico Homes Versus 'Imported' Housing

An older *Tico* house will probably not have en-suite bathrooms; it may not even have hot water throughout. **Kitchens can be tiny** and dark with a cold water sink and simple plywood cabinets.

Even if there is a mountain view in back, you may not have a picture window taking advantage of it. You will likely get a patch of garden and front porch for people watching and either a car port or garage for one car.

Some have likened viewing *Tico* properties to caving! Letting in all that tropical sunshine and light is not part of the *Tico* architectural tradition and rooms can be distinctly gloomy, especially when paneled in dark tropical woods. Having said that, it is a matter of spending time well laced with patience and courtesy to go and see for yourself.

Many gringos live in *Tico* neighborhoods in charming houses and pay under US$400 for the privilege! Rents obviously depend on what you want but you can find a two-bedroom, two-bathroom house with garage for as little as US$400 or go to full luxury extremes for US$4,000 for a fully loaded American-style mansion!

Brokers talk about **the Golden Triangle** to the west of San José. This is an area that roughly falls within the Escazú, Cariari, Rohrmoser districts. Escazú, traditionally, has been a favorite hangout for gringos for years and it is now suffering a backlash reaction caused by its own success and entrepreneurial greed. Clogged streets and uncontrolled development, noisy night spots and exorbitant rents have caused people to look elsewhere.

Cariari, near the international airport, has a golfing resort estate popular with foreigners and lies near the main *autopista* for easy access into San José, the airport or the Pacific coast. Rohrmoser remains an upper-class *Tico*-foreign residential area of over 25-years' standing and here you will find older, independent houses more than condos or gated-community developments.

If you are planning on renting a home, **think unfurnished.** Unless you are looking for *ultra-luxurious* it is difficult to find a well-furnished rental. Please note that when we say unfurnished that's exactly what we mean. You will probably need to buy a refrigerator, chairs, oven and bed as these are rarely included. I have seen places where you would even need to buy all your own light-bulbs.

Rents are certainly higher within the Golden Triangle, but let's get an idea of what *Tico*-style houses are fetching in both this area and in the less fashionable neighborhoods around San José. These are not luxury houses. Upper-end housing will start at around US$1,500 and can reach US$4,000 for a four-to-five-bedroom, full-amenities family house or condo with recreation area, pool and maybe Jacuzzi. This may not be for you or your budget.

Renting In The Golden Triangle – Standard Housing

Obviously by just looking at the newspaper stats, you don't get an idea of the house, its condition or its location. This is just one day's worth in the country's biggest daily newspaper, *La Nación*, but it illustrates what is available to Costa Ricans and they have no intention of paying 'gringo prices'.

- Cariari, Condo, 2 beds, 2 1/2 baths, pool, security, US$600
- Escazú near Anonos, 4 beds, 2 1/2 baths, 2-car garage, 350 m2 (3,766 ft2) construction, US$1,000
- Escazú in Vista de Oro zone, 3 beds, 1 bath, garage, 220 m2 land (2,367 ft2), US$500 unfurnished, US$595 furnished.
- Escazú, 3 beds, 2 baths, 3-car parking, 220 m2 (2,367 ft2) construction, 240 m2 land 2,582 ft2), alarm system, US$675
- Rohrmoser, 3 beds, 1 bath, garage, near to US Embassy, US$310

- Rohrmoser, 4 beds, 4 baths, 2-car garage, patio with BBQ, alarm system, US$700
- Rohrmoser, Condo, 3 beds, 2 1/2 baths, 2-car garage, new US$575

And **outside of the Golden Triangle?** Currently, Heredia is one of the fastest-growing residential and commercial zones in Central Valley. This university town has excellent bargains, its own malls, schools and health care and entertainment centers

- Heredia, San Rafael, 3 beds, 2 baths, garage, 90 m2 (968 ft2) construction, 396 m2 land (4,260 ft2), tiled floor, almost new, US$230
- Heredia, 3 beds, 2 1/2 baths, 2-car garage, US$450
- Belén, Ribera, 3 beds, 1 bath, garage, gardens, US$412
- Coronado, San Antonio, 3 beds, 1 bath, garage, safe, cable TV big patio, US$228
- Curridabat, Lomas del Sol, 3 beds, 1 1/2 baths, 2- car garage, gardens, private security, 2 floors, US$340
- Curridabat, 2 beds, garage, 2 floors, garden, 24 hour guard, US$285
- Guadalupe, 4 beds, 2 baths, 2-car garage, patio and wraparound veranda, US$228
- Moravia, 3 beds, 2 baths, 2 floors, garage, gardens, US$600

If you rent a home, your landlord cannot increase your rent by more than 15% per annum if you pay in colones, (unless inflation increases more than 15%). If you are paying your rent in US dollars, the law does not allow for an annual increase at all. You pay what was agreed upon in your rental agreement for the entire rental period, which is no less than three years.

Leasing

Lease options as part of a purchase deal are possible. If you would like to buy a house but want to be quite sure that the area is right for you, then try to get a lease and have part of the rental money go towards the purchase price. Conversely, if the property you want to buy has tenants renting or leasing it, there could be problems in evicting them so you could wait a long time before you can move in yourself.

Urban leasehold (*Contrato de inquilinato*) is not registered under the property so the only way to find out whether people are renting it is to physically inspect the property and talk to anyone who looks as if they are living there.

Civil Lease (*Arrendamiento Civil*) is regulated by the civil code and is much more limited in its contractual obligations. They are often found with farms and may (or may not) be registered.

Before you even start to think seriously about deciding on which home to rent, **make sure you see the written rental contract**. You must ensure that what is in the written rental contract is exactly the same as what has been stated to you verbally. This is from personal experience when I was told one thing but when it came time for me to sign, the contract stated something very different.

Chapter Four

Buying

Before we take you through the step-by-step details of buying property in Costa Rica, it is well worth taking a little time to put aside the money and legalities and paperwork and think about you and Costa Rica.

You want to buy land and build or purchase a ready-made home here and chances are you are going to have to deal personally with *Ticos* somewhere along the way.

It is their country after all, and surely one of the reasons you have chosen Costa Rica is because of the acceptance and **friendliness of its people.** You may not speak their language and there is no reason why they should speak yours (although many speak good English) so let's just look at how some cultural awareness from your side can make the whole purchase transaction, and your future life here, go a lot smoother for you.

To find out how motivated a seller might be there are two key questions that you can ask: 1. Why are you selling the property? And 2: How much would you take if I offered all cash?

Eric Liljenstolpe, founder-president of Global Solutions Group, has lived in Costa Rica for over five years and illustrates just how important it is to **respect the cultural customs** of your host countrymen.

For some foreigners, the intercultural adjustment process is almost impossible to come to terms with. If you come in with a *superior-than-thou* attitude, you will never be happy in Costa Rica, or probably anywhere else outside your own cultural confines.

Patience, courtesy and tolerance are fundamental factors in successfully crossing those cultural bridges and if you can heap on some humor too, so much the better!

The Culture Of Closing A Costa Rica Real Estate Deal

Here is Eric's story:

With a sweep of the hand and a cheery *"pase adelante"* (come in), I was invited into the room and offered a nice overstuffed seat in front of the impeccably clean and ornately adorned glass coffee table.

The real estate broker brought us both *cafe* and some cookies while the owner of the property and I got right down to business - right down to the business of talking about his family, where he lived, his hobbies, his favorite soccer team and what he thought about the traffic situation in Costa Rica. We discussed pretty much everything *but* the main reason for our little gathering, which was to determine the sale price for a lot I wanted to purchase from him.

After thirty minutes of chit-chat and the occasional animated exchange about soccer, *confianza* (trust) had been developed, meaning we could start talking numbers. He asked how much I was willing to pay.

I knew I shouldn't just throw out a number, but should begin with a long preamble about how I really needed the property for my future family but how, unfortunately, I had just about no money to spend.

I then put out a number, about **half of the asking price**, and we quickly got back to talking about other things.

If you find a home and wish to *lock up* and protect your offer so that nobody can come in and steal it away from you for a slightly better price there is a rarely used legal tool to help you with this. You can use what's called a **priority reserve** which will protect your offer for 30 days from changes in price or the previously agreed terms but as usual, you need to be working with a knowledgeable attorney.

Another 15 minutes passed before he forwarded a counter offer that was not too far from what I ultimately was shooting for, so I decided to try my luck and proposed a number just under my desired price.

When he came back with my target price, I tried hard to disguise my pleasure and asked him if he was sure he wouldn't take less. We closed the deal in just under an hour and a half, including the 10 minutes actually dedicated to speaking about the land.

This may not be your exact experience when purchasing property in Costa Rica, but it illustrates some important cultural points to consider if you are thinking about finding that dream plot in tropical paradise.

1. **Don't be in a hurry**. It is very important to establish a relationship of trust with your counterpart, or at least the appearance of one. Ask about their family, their needs and desires, what makes them tick. Tell them about yourself as well. Although this rule applies in many countries, it is true to a greater degree in Costa Rica. Take

more time for it than you think is necessary. The negotiations will go more smoothly if you do.

2. **Beware of the violin**. "*Sacando el violin*" literally means "Taking out the violin" and refers to the practice of **playing on your emotions.** *Ticos* often expound on how poor and unfortunate they are as grounds to request a discount. Playing the victim is a very common negotiation technique in Costa Rica. While most people with western-European cultural roots prefer to **avoid showing weakness** and are reluctant to use this strategy, it is very acceptable in Costa Rica and can be used to gain the advantage. Although you should be aware that many sob stories are fabricated, don't forget that these can sometimes be used to your advantage when dealing with your Costa Rican counterpart.

3. **Trust, but double-check**. It is very common, even if you have developed *confianza*, that the seller will tell you whatever you want to hear to make the deal. This is not generally considered to be lying, as it is just **withholding or embellishing the truth**. As a result of practices like this, there is a high degree of distrust within society. In fact, in a recent poll taken throughout Latin America, only 8% of Ticos said they could trust other Costa Ricans, one of the lowest figures in all of Latin America (Latinobarometro, 2004).

4. **Keep your cool.** Even if you discover your counterpart is lying or some other unpleasant detail, don't lose your cool. **Harmony is highly valued** in the Costa Rican culture, and is manifested by maintaining a calm and agreeable exterior, no matter how you feel on the inside.

What kind of culture shock should be expected? How can you prepare yourself? Learn more by reading our articles at

WeLoveCostaRica.com

No hard-and-fast rules apply when dealing with something as complex as a foreign culture. However, these principles might help to deal with unfamiliar behavior.

One of the best and most necessary strategies is still to find a cultural interpreter, someone you can trust who is knowledgeable about the local culture and can let you know what is going on, linguistically as well as culturally.

Our thanks to Eric Liljenstolpe, founder-president of Global Solutions

Group, for his expert information.

It is generally accepted that the **buyer and seller share equally** in the closing costs. You should clarify this before you make a formal offer and it will obviously depend on the specific transaction.

Just Because You Are A Gringo, Does Not Mean You Must Pay "Top Dollar" Prices

Having looked at the cultural differences between *Ticos* and gringos, let's be clear about the term. You hear gringo constantly if you live in Costa Rica and most other Latin American countries too.

Unlike other places, though, **'gringo' is not a derogatory term** and is used just because most people naturally categorize their fellow humans into castes, races or sects. Gringo is liberally applied to any non-*Latinos* although it more precisely refers to North Americans.

Other northern nationalities will sometimes correct the title with a, "No, I'm a Canadian (British or German or whatever)". But, you will hear fellow gringos using the term on themselves so don't feel insulted or feel that it is some kind of racial slur.

More significantly, it does mean in the minds of many *Latinos*, and Costa Ricans are no different, that ***'Gringo Means Money'***. True or not, gringos represent a higher cash flow and capital access than most *Ticos* and if you look at the average minimum wages for the country, you will see why.

The *Caja Costarricense de Seguro Social* (Costa Rica Social Security Department) published the following **minimum monthly wage** guidelines for January 2004:

- *Peon* or an unskilled laborer - US$202
- Specialized industrial worker, truck or bus driver - US$278
- Car driver - US$244. Heavy equipment operator - US$230
- Cook - US$266, waiter - US$233
- Computer operator - US$320. Accountant - US$388
- Clerk, guard, receptionist - US$252
- Maid - US$134 plus food

Don't forget – this is *per month!* No wonder many *Ticos* think it's fair game to boost certain prices for gringos and it certainly applies to real estate.

We said above that there is a marked distinction between what is aimed at the gringo market and the advertisements directed at *Ticos*. As a foreigner visiting with a view to buying or renting, **you will often be shown the fanciest, most expensive** places by a smooth English-speaking broker.

Again, please bear in mind that the average salary in the US, Canada and Europe is significantly higher (probably six times higher) than a comparable salary in Costa Rica where, for example, **a school teacher with 30 years' experience makes about US$1,100 a month**.

So, since *Ticos* know this, it's not that surprising when the occasional Costa Rican property owner asks more for his home when a foreigner or gringo wants to buy it, than he would if another *Tico* wanted to buy it. The *Tico* assumes that all the gringos are rich and therefore "I'll raise my price a little and see what happens."

Closing costs in Costa Rica typically involve three things: government taxes and fees, notary fee, and mortgage costs. Total closing costs on a US$100,000 home will be approximately US$3,773. Make sure you understand exactly what you are due to pay.

Let's not forget that the house **will only sell** for a certain price **if someone is willing to buy it for that price.** If you were in the market to sell your own home and thought that it was worth US$100K but wanted more, asked US$150K for it and someone then offered you US$150K , are you going to turn them down?

Of course not. If a buyer willingly pays the price you're asking for your property, what's the problem? Nobody is forcing them to buy your property at that price.

Whatever the piece of Costa Rica real estate you plan on buying, **you must do your homework!** Unless you know the Costa Rica real estate market intimately, you need to make sure you're dealing with professionals who do know the local market.

The bottom line is simple… **If you don't think the price is right, don't buy it!** Say *"Adios"* and move on to the next place. There's no shortage of beautiful properties for sale in Costa Rica.

So How Do You Avoid The Money-Hungry Brokers?

There are plenty of bargains out there. It's just that many of them are advertised in Spanish and directed at the local populace. However, don't be put off and simply give in to the English-speaking brokers and English-language information sources - **it is not that hard** to decipher the Spanish ads in the Classifieds of the daily newspapers.

Most *Ticos* are simply not in the market for the top-end luxury homes, so where do they look when it comes to finding a new house? Many of them will naturally use their family and neighborhood networks to find out about places through word of mouth. But you don't have the language, so how else can you get loads of inside information?

The country is awash with land and properties for sale - there is plenty of choice, and one of the best and simplest sources for finding out about them *Tico*-style, is through the country's biggest daily newspaper, *La Nación*.

Some homes have hot water in the kitchen but not in the bathroom and it's here you'll discover the strangest showerhead you've ever seen in your life. It's one of those showerheads that heats the water in the head before it showers you. They are ugly, not particularly effective and some people consider them downright dangerous which is why they are called *suicide showers.*

By clicking onto **economicos.com/navigate.do** you can see what the *Ticos* search for. If you were to visit these same areas with that smart but unscrupulous English-speaking broker, you wouldn't even be shown some of the properties but if you were, count on it, the prices could be very different.

If it's a bargain you are looking for, there are plenty more days in the year, plenty more editions of the paper to peruse, and you could well find your ideal home this way.

The best day for studying *La Nación* is Saturday when it publishes its *Metro Cuadrado - M2* (Square Meter) pull-out section that is packed with real estate articles and a comprehensive classified listing of properties for sale or rent. But don't take our word for it. Click onto **economicos.com/navigate.do** and using the Spanish - English glossary at the end of this report, start researching for yourself!

If you are not bothered about living in a smart, fashionable gringo area, with landscaped gardens, fully fitted kitchen or marble bathrooms and pool in the yard (with a price tag to match) then **you can find some real bargains.**
If you have looked over the Renting section, **Rents You Can Expect To Pay and Where**, then you have an idea of how prices can differ.

You Do Not Understand Spanish?

No problem! That doesn't have to stop you even though it's all in Spanish, and abbreviated Spanish at that! Using the complete glossary at the end of *How To Buy Costa Rica Real Estate Without Losing Your Camisa*, try working out the terminology. Like the classifieds back home, they repeat notations and abbreviations with general location, size, price and other details.

Once you have your short list, it's time to find a Spanish-speaking friend who can travel around with you and help you through the verbal intricacies of house hunting in *Tiquicia*.

La Nación's property Classifieds are broken down into rental, sales and purchase of apartments, houses, condos, farms, offices, warehouses - just about all categories are included.

The classifieds deal mostly with San José and the main Central Valley settlements (Cartago, Atenas, Grecia, Heredia, Alajuela), although special real estate editions are regularly produced that include other regions, especially the Pacific coast.

Interested in buying or building **a log home** in Costa Rica? You can learn more by reading our articles at **WeLoveCostaRica.com**

Quick-View Guide To Land And Property Prices

As with the section on **Renting**, here you can have a look over some land and property prices as calculated in September, 2004.

San José. Property in San José seems to be appreciating at 3% p.a. Land - US$75 - 150 m2 ($7 – 14 ft2).

- Golden Triangle (Escazú, Cariari, Rohrmoser): Land - US$100 - 300 m2 ($9.3 – 27.8 ft2)
  Standard house - 2/3 beds US$150,000 to US$500,000
  Luxury house - US$250,000 - US$1,200,000
  Condominium - US$100,000 to US$800,000
- San Pedro and Los Yoses (near University of Costa Rica, these older residential neighborhoods now have restaurants, night spots and malls):
  Land - US$100 - 300 m2 ($9.3 – 27.8 ft2)
  Standard house - US$100,000 - US$500,000
- Moravia, Coronado, Guadalupe (older residential areas, now less popular than the western districts but with malls and general

amenities):

Land - US$50 - 200 m2 ($4.6 – 18.5 ft2)

Standard house - US$100,000 - US$250,000

- Cartago and area (cooler climate in mountains, steep road access in areas):

Land - US$25 - 100 m2 ($2.3 – 9.3 ft2)

Standard house (Cartago) - US$60,000 - US$80,000; (Turrialba) - US$40,000 - US$60,000

- Santa Ana / Ciudad Colón (growth area of old farming communities with new malls and amenities):

Land - US$50 m2 ($4.6 ft2)

Standard to luxury house - US$150,000 - US$550,000

- Heredia (the booming area of the moment):

Land - (downtown) US$100 - 300 m2 ($9.3 – 27.8 ft2) (*Tico* neighborhoods) US$20 m2 (41.8 ft2) (Upper class areas and higher up the hill) US$50 ($4.6 ft2) or more m2

Standard 3 bed house - US$80,000 and up

- Alajuela:

Land - (downtown) US$100 - 300 m2 ($9.3 – 27.8 ft2); (outside) US$25 m2 ($2.3 ft2)

Houses - US$70,000 - US$300,000

Weekend homes (in hills above) - US$150,000 - US$500,000

- La Garita & Atenas (popular for great climate, weekend restaurants and hotels):

Land - (downtown) US$20 - 50 m2 ($1.8 – 4.6 ft2); (rural areas) US$75 - 200 m2 ($7 – 18.5 ft2)

Standard houses/weekend houses - US$75,000 - US$500,000

Costa Rica introduced stringent emissions testing in June 2000 for used cars and motorcycles imported into Costa Rica. This applied to all used vehicles regardless of whether they are driven or shipped into the country, for permanent or temporary use by their owners. This law required that emissions testing takes place two months BEFORE you ship it or drive it into Costa Rica. Few people realize it but **this has been changed** and you can now get the car tested AFTER it's in the country.

How To Calculate Value

According to the Costa Rica Chamber of Real Estate Brokers (*Camera Costarricense de Corredores de Bienes Raices* - CCCBR), a property can have differing values depending on who is doing the evaluation. Five main categories apply that you should be aware of before agreeing to a sales price:

- **Asking Price** - The owner wants to get the highest possible price for the property, but don't forget that this is a culture where **bargaining is a commonly accepted practice.** Even though you know there is always some haggling over the price, here it can become a battle of nerves to settle on a price that suits you.

- **Comparative Value** - Data on recently sold properties with similar characteristics in comparative zones are collected to provide parameters to work out an estimate of price.

- **Investment Value** - The property is appraised for its potential worth and future income capacity to estimate the price an investor would spend in today's market.

- **Replacement Value** - The site is valued and the cost of replacing the standing construction with a new one is added. Depreciation is factored in if there is an older building on site to give this value.

- **Actual Value** - "**It's only worth what someone is prepared to pay for it**". Simply, this is the closing price that a buyer is happy to pay to a seller.

If you decide to build your own house, you can refer to standardized budget tables listing costs of materials and labor. Construction companies and engineers use them to calculate value for their clients.

For peace of mind in buying a home in Costa Rica you may wish to consider working with a title guaranty company. They will guarantee property titles registered in the Costa Rican National Registry (*Registro Nacional*) against defects in the title. There can be major differences between title companies. One company we prefer offers coverage for certain defects of title, even if these do not appear on the registered title or cannot be detected during normal due diligence title searches and/or investigations conducted in the ordinary course of legal business. Visit **WeLoveCostaRica.com** and click on Contact Us if you need more information.

However, if your top-quality, luxury home is constructed in an area with little demand, you could end up losing on your investment when you come to sell it. However intense your hard-sales act, you won't sell the place or cover your costs.

Once again, before you commit and start pouring out money, get good advice from professionals who know their market.

Simple Way To Assess Property

It boils down to value being what the building costs and price, what someone is willing to pay for it. However, here is a quick way to get an idea of what property might be worth:

- How many square meters make up the property?

- How many square meters of construction?

- How old is the building? Has it been remodeled? Any other added value?

The value of a construction is broken down into three broad price ranges:

- US$500 – 600 per m2 ($46.5 – 55.7 ft2) for low/medium quality. Simple design, aluminum windows without colors, simple agglomerated doors, partially tiled bathrooms, electric garage doors, internal gypsum walls.

- US$600 – 700 per m2 ($55.7 – 65 ft2) for medium quality. Quality finishing, quality ceramics, internal gypsum walls with colored aluminum windows, wooden doors, melamine kitchen surfaces with wood kitchen cabinets, bathrooms tiled to 1.20m.

- US$750 + per m2 ($70 ft2) for high/luxury quality. External and internal walls in concrete. Quality ceramic flooring, solid wood doors and frames, designed ceilings with cornice, wood baseboards, kitchen with granite counters, bathrooms lined in marble with tub or Jacuzzi, laminated wood floors in bedrooms.

Real estate and financial services in Costa Rica are **not well regulated.** There are con men in every country and unfortunately, many people have lost serious money in a variety of investment 'programs' in Costa Rica. **Don't leave your brain on the plane** when it comes to evaluating investments. Do your homework! Check things out carefully and remember that many of the scam artists you will come across are Americans and Canadians, not Costa Ricans. If in doubt, visit **WeLoveCostaRica.com** and click on Contact Us.

Let's take a look at one example:

A good quality ten-year-old, 325-m2 (3,500 ft2) house with modern ceramic floors, wooden doors, good quality kitchen and well-preserved infrastructure with a total land area of 800 m2 (8,608 ft2). The land value for that neighborhood is at US$100 m2 ($9.3 ft2) and the cost of "medium" quality construction is about US$600 m2 ($55.7 ft2).

Multiply 325 x US$600 = US$195,000 less 10 years at 2% p.a. (10 x 2 = 20% = US$39,000).

The value of construction is US$195,000 less US$39,000 = US$156,000. Add land value of 800 x US$100 = US$80,000 to construction value (US$156,000) to give total value of US$236,000.

Say the property was remodeled four years ago at a cost of US$20,000. Deduct 4 x 2% from the US$20,000 (US$8% = US$1,600), which should give you an added value of US$18,400. This is added to the total property value for a final total of US$254,000.

This provides at least **a ball-park figure** for calculating house values in urban areas.

Foreigners (but not of the same sex) can be married in Costa Rica. Both civil marriages, performed by a judge, mayor, provincial governor, or a public notary, and marriages performed by a priest in the Catholic Church are recognized. Individuals of other religious denominations, must resort to a civil ceremony. The rights and obligations of the matrimony take effect when the declaration of marriage is registered in the National Civil Registry.

How The Municipal Authority Assesses Property Values

The municipal government assesses property values to calculate tax rates, where the property is appraised in three ways:

1. **Voluntary Declaration:** The municipal government sends out a voluntary declaration inviting the property owner to complete it and return it to the municipal office. Some municipal governments have developed databases for property prices in their area and they expect the owner to adhere to those established values when filing the declaration. This is **the most common method in the San José** metropolitan areas.

2. **Municipal Appraisal:** If the property owner does not file a voluntary declaration, the municipal government may send out their appraisal staff to the property and have it appraised and taxed based on that appraisal.

3. **Property Transfer or Mortgage:** Another appraisal method is the municipal government checking the last property transaction. If you transfer property or place a mortgage on it, the tax basis for the property will be adjusted

upwards to the value stated in the transfer deed or mortgage.

Some Secrets On Buying Affordable Land

Now you have seen what some prices fetch per square meter you can understand that buying from a developer in a *hot* area, means paying premium prices for your land.

It makes good sense to **choose your area carefully** and, though there might be some shortcomings in infrastructure, they can bring the prices right down. The obvious difference between *Tico* properties and housing aimed for the foreign market is one aspect, but other considerations might just turn the price in your favor:

- Distance from the main road.

- Serviced by a public bus route.

- Cable TV or computer hook-up available.

- Mains water installed or is well water available?

If you don't mind not having these services, then search accordingly and you could well find some bargain plots of land.

Russ Martin is an internet marketing consultant living in Coronado, east of San José. This isn't in the Golden Triangle so he has immediately avoided some of the inflated asking prices for property. Coronado is a traditional *Tico* residential area and he has lived there since 1996.

Stay away from untitled property; it's a legal minefield.

He has the advantage in that his wife is *Tica*, which opens up the family network and means language is never a hurdle. Here, he shares nine hot tips to finding a bargain based on location, tradeoffs and opportunities.

- **Look for opportunities – with a *Tico!*** Have a *Tico* friend help you search for places. Either look up the ads in *La Nación* newspaper or drive around an area of your choice and have your friend ask local watchmen or shopkeepers about property for sale. (Don't forget to carry the **Glossary Of Terms** along with you!) Because it is a buyers' market just now, it is worth waiting for a good deal to come along. Someone may have to sell for health or financial reasons and you will be able to negotiate a good price.

- **Where to look?** Russ recommends looking at rural areas such as Atenas or around Tibás on the highway to Limón. Many farmers are selling land **at very reasonable rates**; however, although access to San José is good if you have a car, it is remote if you need to rely on buses.

- **Build high quality at affordable prices.** With a current investment of US$59,701 for a 210 m2 (2,259 ft2) home on 2,800 m2 (30,128 ft2) of land with a rustic guest house of 48 m2 (516 ft2) with fireplace and loft, Russ calculates his per-meter average cost. Subtracting the investment in land and the guest cabin (US$20,795) from the total US$59,701, he divides the remaining US$38,906 by 210 m2s for a US$185.26 per square meter on his home ($17.2 per square foot)! That is way cheaper than many developers who charge from US$500 to US$900 per square meter ($46.5 – 83.6 ft2) in the Golden Triangle areas.

- **Build for the tropics.** You can build a high-quality home but it may not be a *gringo* home. These are the tropics and some things you can do without. Hot water may only be necessary in the showers and bath tubs. Dishes are washed in cold water, without a dishwasher. Expensive air conditioning units or central heating can be left out too.

- **Is building best for you?** Building is not for everyone. Even in the US or Europe most people who build their own homes, do it only once! So if you decide to go ahead in a foreign country with a different language and culture, think twice. **You will need either experience in construction and/or Spanish** – preferably both.

Russ built his rustic guest cabin, working as a laborer to gain practice in building techniques. Although he didn't work on the main house, he spoke Spanish and helped supervise based on his experiences. He and his *Tica* wife also lived in the guest cabin during construction of the main house and could keep a close eye on quality and materials.

When you eat out in restaurants in Costa Rica the tip is nearly always included in the check. You may see *Impto. Servicio*, or *Imp. Servicio* or *I. SERV* at the bottom of your check or bill which is an abbreviation for *Impuesto Servicio* or Service Charge. If your waiter was particularly attentive, you may wish to give a little extra (10%), which will always be greatly appreciated.

- **Never include materials in the building contract.** When and if you build, accept that there will be delays. Delays mean money and some contractors will skimp on materials to maintain their profit margin. They will still ask for more money in the end anyway as most miscalculate on the original estimate and time frame for completion. There is also the risk that materials are purchased that somehow never quite make it to your building site!

- **Never pay by the hour.** Paying by the hour brings frustration. Progress may be slowed down to pad out the hours. Be prepared to pay your contractor a fair price with a fair profit for him. Once you get some estimates and construction has started, you will have an idea how long the whole process will take.

- **Buy your materials personally and check delivery.** If you pay cash at the building depot, you almost always get up to 10% discount over paying by credit or debit card for anything other than basic materials. So ask for a list of materials your contractor needs and go look for estimates.

  If you choose one depot or hardware store, you will get a better price if you commit to them for the entire process. Remember to factor in delivery costs; it pays to find somewhere as close to your site as possible.

  It is a good idea to ask the site foreman for his list of materials around lunchtime each day. This gives you time to call in the afternoon and arrange for next morning delivery.

- **Is it worth it?** Russ reckons that labor costs depend on the length of building contract. A contractor looking at a 160-m2 (1,721-ft2) house over a six-month period can charge less per week than being asked to build a 50-m2 (538-ft2) extension over four weeks. But with the US$ exchange-rate variables, the difference per week between 1997 and 2004 for one contractor and three helpers was US$321 as opposed to US$300!

  The wildcard is the fluctuation of materials and price of crude oil as this is seriously affecting certain materials such as steel. Transport costs too are climbing sharply and will affect overall construction costs.

Interested in building an **income-producing property** in Costa Rica? You can learn more by reading our articles at **WeLoveCostaRica.com**

Buying For Investment

Most people buy a house because they want a roof over their heads ᵤ.
call home, and without putting too much thought into it, they also hope ᵢ.
will increase in value when the time comes to sell.

Others, however, buy for purely investment purposes with no intention of living in the property, or they buy raw land without planning to develop it in the hope that land prices in the chosen area will rise.

But none of us wants to see the huge outlay we have made on buying property come to nothing, so for the majority of us it comes down to a compromise of balancing our dreams of an ideal home against considerations that a property should increase in value and have a profitable resale capability.

Just because your builder, plumber or other contractor says he will start work at 8 am doesn't mean he'll be there. Many contractors will tell you something they know is not quite true because they don't want to disappoint you. Another example of this is asking someone in the street for directions: even if they don't know the way, they will still give you directions because they simply don't want to disappoint you. (There are some things in life you just shouldn't dwell on!)

You may still be weighing up the pros and cons of investing in Costa Rica real estate. Maybe you aren't sure it is a wise investment and without having all the details it might be too risky. So, why invest in Costa Rica?

Many people have been understandably frightened by what has happened in the global financial markets over the last five years or so. For a big percentage of these investors, the stock market has not been profitable and many have turned to **real estate for more solid, long-term investments**.

- Low bank rates mean **cheaper loans** and that's good news for anyone wanting to build or buy.

- A huge number of North American, Canadian and European *Baby Boomers* will reach retirement age and looking around for pleasant, secure retirement properties, not necessarily in their home countries but over the entire world. Costa Rica can offer a **quality of life** that fits the bill in many ways.

- Costa Rica's tradition of **peace and democracy** is passionately defended by its people. It has a well-earned reputation for being stable and safe - good investment factors.

...etters the care offered in America or ...per.

...olleges can give your children a first-class, ...ecognized education at a fraction the cost back

...hotel companies and development corporations are heavily ...ived in internationally backed resort development and mega-...ourism projects in Costa Rica. They have no intention of seeing a loss on their investment. If they are prepared to go ahead, why don't you?

Want to **live on the beach**? You can read about the 23 positives and 23 negatives in our articles at **WeLoveCostaRica.com**

What Are My Rights?

As a foreigner, you have virtually the same rights as a Costa Rican to rent, purchase and develop land. And fortunately for you, in Costa Rica, there is a defined process through which a careful buyer and builder can proceed. The main difference arises if you want to invest in beachfront property (see the section on **Life On The Beach**).

Everyone is allowed to go to the *Registro Nacional* (National Property Registry) and look through any registered title deeds to check ownership, boundaries, liens or any other detail you would like to have on a particular property. It is a free public service.

Just remember that there are different departments covering different aspects (survey plans, company-owned property, beach property, condominiums, etc.) and these have to be researched one by one. You can also check online at **registronacional.go.cr** (see section on **The *Registro Nacional***) but this is a Spanish-only site.

Owning property is your constitutional right – in theory. The Law on Expropriation cites that your land might be expropriated without compensation in times of war or civil unrest. A slightly more serious risk of expropriation could arise if your land was needed in the interests of the public good and the *Instituto Costarricense de Energia* - ICE (Costa Rican Department of Energy) is known to wield the full weight of its monopoly might to steamroller decisions their way if they decide they need some or all of your land for their own purposes.

Officially, they, or any other government department need a two-thirds in-favor vote by the legislature and justification that it is in the public interest (such as a hydro-electric project or new highway).

Before losing your property, the government is obliged to pay you a cash indemnity. Reality is often different and compensation payments take years to materialize. (See the section on **Expropriation**.)

However, without dwelling on such unlikely events, as a property owner you are entitled to:

- possession, which can be individual (*personalmente*) or joint (*en copropiedad*) when two or more people equally own a property; in trust (*en fideicomiso*) or in the name of a company or corporation (*en nombre de una compañia*);

- benefit from whatever the land can provide (except for minerals that are owned by the government);

- alter the land or transfer it;

- defend your land from trespass;

- claim restitution of the land and indemnity for damages resulting from dispossession, as long as your land is legally registered in your name.

There are only a few dangerous animals in Costa Rica, although you will probably never come across one in your everyday life. There are poisonous snakes, the deadliest of which is the fer de lance or *Bothrops asper*. But, if you do see this beauty, **there's no need to panic**, just calmly leave the area!

Buying As A Company Or Corporation

There are several reasons why you might wish to purchase your property in the name of a company:

- You remain **fairly anonymous.**

- Your personal assets are not held responsible for any costs that could arise from the property.

- If you get into serious debt, **you won't lose the house** if it's in a company name, as a personal asset to pay back the debt.

- You can put the company shares into your children's or spouse's names and **avoid probate** in case of your demise.

- You **avoid the transfer tax** on the future sale of the property since the buyer can simply buy the shares of the company that holds the property. This is also a **quicker way** to expedite the transfer. Obviously, the company should have no liabilities that would also be passed onto the buyer.

- **All companies must file an income tax return.** If there has been no movement in the company and it is being used purely as a holding company for the property, you will only have to pay the annual stamp duty and the property tax which is 0.25% of the registered tax value.

Forewarned is forearmed. Want to prepare and learn more about Costa Rica attorneys? You can by reading our articles at **WeLoveCostaRica.com**

There Are Two Types Of Company Available

Corporations (*Sociedad Anónima*) You must have at least **three board members** (who don't have to be resident in Costa Rica) plus a fiscal and agent resident in the country (who must also be an attorney). If the corporation is purely a holding company for the property, you pay no tax. Only a yearly stamp (*Timbre de Educación y Cultura*) of between US$3 – 25 is due. There is **no capital gains tax** so any transfer of stock is not taxable either.

Limited Company (*Sociedad de Responsabilidad Limitada*). This is a less-used option. Only one manager is needed but all shareholders must agree to any transfer of shares (*cuotas*).

Starting up a company with a name of your choice can take some time and if you wish to move more quickly, you could buy a ready-made corporation that has already been incorporated but which has had no commercial activity. If you decide to do this, then check that the company is free from any liabilities and has indeed had no activity prior to you taking it on.

If you would like more detailed information about setting up a corporation, a Panama foundation or even a Costa Rican trust, please visit **WeLoveCostaRica.com** and then click on Contact Us.

Portofino

Chapter Five

The Purchase Process

Inspect Before You Buy

Yes, things are a little different down here and surveying a property before buying is just one of the differences that can cause many foreign purchasers a lot of anxiety.

Not having this service readily available, or even a required part of the purchase process, is a bit scary if you aren't a technical person yourself and could just turn you off buying altogether.

Most buyers who move for the first time to Costa Rica are unfamiliar with the building techniques and are confused about certain features, especially in older *Tico*-style homes. The typical water pump installations or *suicide showers* you can find in homes without a normal water heater are a case in point.

A suicide shower is where the electric shower heater mounts directly above the shower head and often has a knife switch on the wall nearby. Many gringos are not used to seeing sometimes live and unprotected electric wires near to a water outlet.

Potential buyers may not know if the home has a septic tank system or whether it is tied to the municipal drainage system and are often really perplexed about the typically disorganized and visible household wiring. As for those cracks in the walls, they may wonder if the house is stable or not.

You should **look with suspicion upon any 'appraisal'** given to you by the seller. It may well be accurate but you must do your own homework.

Household pests such as mice, spiders, scorpions, termites and bats are other considerations that may need eradicating.

California born Jere McKinney has set up a home-inspection business to help out first-time buyers in Costa Rica by offering his expert eye to survey new properties for clients.

Jere provides the service with a comprehensive written report on all aspects of the property in question, both good and bad. His services are in demand since in the past only an informal building contractor's verbal opinion was available.

A typical inspection can take three hours for a two-to-three bedroom house. Then another day to organize and write up the report with all useful information included, such as where to find the main shut-off valves for the street water system, the location of drain cleanouts and the septic tank system.

Jere's home-inspection **rates are reasonable** and it's important to note that the final report could be a great tool to help you **negotiate a better price** from the seller. The cost of an inspection is trivial compared to the **staggering expenses** you might face if you buy the wrong property.

Either way, **a home inspection is a smart move** when you are serious about making an offer on a property.

The **prices below** are for inspection of a single building under 500 m2 (5,380 ft2) in the Central Valley area. Outside the metropolitan area and for multiple buildings, special rates can be negotiated.

- Up to 150 m2. Minimum price US$200
- 151 m2s to 300 m2 = US$250
- 301 m2s to 400 m2 = US$350
- 401 m2s to 500 m2 = US$400

Our thanks to Jere McKinney for his expert information about home inspections. If you would like more detailed information about home inspections, please visit **WeLoveCostaRica.com** and click on Contact Us.

There are approximately 50,000 Europeans, Canadians and Americans living in Costa Rica. Only a few of them speak Spanish but thankfully many Costa Ricans do speak English. However, when it comes to legal contracts, **make sure that you understand every single word** of the document you are signing. For a minimal additional cost, you can always have everything translated.

Step By Step – The Legal Stuff

Before you commit to buying, the **first, most important step** you can take is to choose an attorney. Don't listen to any assurances from the sellers about using their lawyer to save money. You will be leaping into a barrel of problems if you do, however much *trust* has been established.

A good attorney who **specializes in real estate** should help ensure that the contract best serves your needs and interests and he will protect you throughout the whole transaction process.

The basic legal steps you will go through when buying a property are:

- Check that **your personal papers are in order**. You will need your identification card (*cédula*) or passport for any legal transaction so it makes sense to confirm they are not out of date or missing the correct stamp.

- Find the property you want to buy and negotiate the purchase price and conditions through your broker, if you have used one. Find out **how the seller expects** purchase payments to be made. You will almost certainly be expected to make a deposit of good faith to be held against completion of purchase.

- Have the seller put **in writing** everything to be included with the property, especially if pre-closing documents are to be made up and signed.

- Get a registered plot map (*plano catastrado*) from the National Registry (*Registro Nacional*) clearly showing that the property you want and what you get is the same!

- If the map is outdated, have a topographer re-survey the plot. Plot maps are registered in the Map Registry (*Catastro*) department in the Property Registry of the *Registro Nacional*.

- Get the registration number or *matricula de folio real* of the property from the *Registro Nacional*. This unique identification number is key to finding the information you need. To understand the coding system: The *folio real* number goes before the province number (123456-1 = number 123456 in San José Province). After another hyphen, you will find a sub-registration indicating the number of people with rights to the property (001 or 002, for example).

The reason you see so many foreigners with books is because they know some everyday errands can take time. You would be advised to always **have a good book on hand** just in case of delays at the bank or when you apply for your driving license.

- Do a search (*estudio*) of the public records for ownership (individual or corporation), property location, boundary lines, registered survey, liens, encumbrances, declared value of property and any other annotations that can affect the transfer.

- If the seller insists on a pre-closing or earnest money deposit, **don't be bullied into rushing!** It might give them security that you won't back out of the deal but it also forces your hand to close sooner than you may be ready to do so. One option is to place any money in trust or escrow with your attorney, **never with the seller**.

- The transfer deed (*escritura*) is drawn up and signed by vendor, buyer and notary.

- The deed is recorded in the notary's record book with a copy presented to the *Registro* for registration.

- Once the notary places the deed with the Registry, it can be annotated. This is a note to state the deed is in the process of being registered and it takes precedence over any other documents that might be presented.

- The *Registro* checks the deed, making any necessary corrections and it is registered under the new owner's name. The deed must be presented immediately to benefit from the three-months' protection that no other deed or limiting documentation can be presented that could affect the property.

- Payment is made of all due taxes, stamps and notary fees.

- Once all payments and fees are paid and all conditions met, the deed must be registered within one year of presentation, otherwise it will be voided.

- **Check that the deed is registered** by getting a copy of the closing document (*testimonio*) signed by the registrar and its computerized entry or *certificación* naming you or your company as legal owners.

That's it! Once the deeds are registered in your name, you need no other documents. It is advisable, of course, to make copies or have a notary certify your ownership and **keep everything in a very safe place**!

Would you like to have your own swimming pool on your property? Find out what to look out for by reading our articles at **WeLoveCostaRica.com**

Survey Maps

All property should have a registered map with the owner's name and a reference number in the *Catastro* or *Mapeo* registry. It will be marked on a master map and should indicate its size and boundaries in relation to surrounding properties, so you can see the exact location of your land. Since May, 1999, all transfer deeds must have a survey map reference number.

The *Registro* will not register the deeds without one.

Some notaries will not check that the piece of land or property you have seen and want to buy is in fact the same as the supposed land on the survey map accompanying the purchase papers.

Obviously, **it is in your interests to verify this** and if you have doubts, contract an independent surveyor to help. It is also possible that information indicated on the survey map may differ from that in the *Registro* report.

How does this happen? All property is registered by the notary to indicate the right of possession. However, the survey map can be modified by the owner and changes may not necessarily be reflected in the registered deeds. Changes might include new pathways, topographical corrections, adjusted measurements or even a different owner from that found on the deeds.

> Believe it or not, Costa Rica has fairly stringent building codes; the problem is that these codes are rarely enforced in rural areas. Play it safe and play by the rules or you may have problems selling.

Staking Out Boundary Lines (*Replanteo*)

When buying a property **we recommend that all buyers do a *replanteo*** – which basically means a surveyor comes out and physically opens up boundary lines two-to-four meters (6.5 – 13 feet) wide, placing stakes to mark the property lines. The cost for doing this can range from US$300 to US$1,000, depending on the size of the property.

Why Should You Do This?

Most owners **do not know** their exact property lines and the law does not require them to be marked. The real estate agent you are dealing with will probably only know what the owner told him and as you now know, that information may well be incorrect!

If you are a careful and prudent buyer (which you are if you are reading this book), we would recommend you spend a little extra money and be *100%*

sure about what exactly you are agreeing to buy.

Some people seem to think it's the obligation of the seller to pay for this; it is not. It would be good if the seller agrees to pay for the *replanteo,* but normally, the job will get done a lot quicker if you, the buyer, arrange and pay for the *replanteo.*

Getting Registered!

Getting that evidence of registration is VITAL! If your deeds are not registered in the *Registro* within one year, they will be considered null and void and the previous owner could resell your property. If a subsequent buyer were to register before you do, your unregistered deeds are worth nothing.

Once all transfer fees are paid, the Notary will present (*anotar*) and register (*inscribir*) the transfer in the Property Section of the *Registro Nacional.* You should **check to make sure** the registration has been done and not just shelved for a later date that may never happen.

Once registered, the Registry returns all original documentation duly stamped and sealed. This should be completed about one month after presentation.

Check Your Registration Occasionally

You might want to periodically check your registration in the *Registro Público* section of the *Registro Nacional* to satisfy yourself that no liens have been placed on your property subsequent to registration. Although rare, there have been cases of **unscrupulous characters** posing as representatives of owners, selling property to well-meaning third parties, by forging powers of attorney in your name. You can make these checks yourself or, by paying a subscription fee, you can access the data online at **registronacional.go.cr**

More About The *Registro Nacional*

All property must be recorded in the relevant property section of the *Registro Público* (Public Registry) in the *Registro Nacional* (National Registry) as per Article 460 of the Civil Code. It might surprise you but in fact, **99% of all properties are registered.**

Condominiums are registered in their own special section called *Propiedad Horizontal* and beach properties are registered in a special section called *Registro de Concesiones de la Zona Marítimo Terrestre.* All properties must have a unique title registration number, the *folio real* or *matricula.*

Putting up a glossy Website with great photographs of luxurious properties and promising a *happy ever after* is easy to do. It does not necessarily make the site an 'expert' source of real estate.

The *informe registral,* or Public Registry Report will tell you the name of the title holder, boundary lines, property tax appraisal, declared value, liens, encumbrances, mortgages, recorded easements and other details that might affect title. You will have to go to the corresponding registries in the *Registro* to get this information:

- Mortgages (*Hipoteca*);

- Bond mortgages (*Cedulas Hipotecarias*);

- Condominiums (*Propiedad Horizontal*);

- Commercial (*Sección Mercantil*);

- Beachfront (*Concesiones de la Zona Marítimo Terrestre*);

- Public Works Concessions (*Registro de Concesiones de Obra Pública*);

- Plot or Cadaster registry (*catastro*);

- Leases (*Arrendamientos*);

- Transfer journal (*Diario*) - all documents not yet registered but presented;

- Scanning department (*Escaneo*);

- Maps (*Mapeo*);

- *Personas* - register of powers of attorney and anyone affected by outstanding liens or conditions.

The final transfer of deed is registered here. You can access this information either with a personal visit to the Registry or check the status of the real estate that you are interested online at **registronacional.go.cr** A few properties are not registered online meaning you will have to go down and look through the *tomos* or folio volumes.

> **Property taxes are minimal.** There are some exceptions but the property tax rate is usually only 0.25% of the recorded value of the property.

Your real estate **attorney should do this** on your behalf. However, not all properties have accurate data on land titles because there is no complete overall register of land surveys. It is important to check with all the registries. The National Cadaster registry handles individual plot maps for each property being processed but the maps don't always tally with neighboring maps.

That can cause trouble when it comes to recorded titles. At the time of writing, plans are being finalized to completely update the whole legal system for real estate records. This will make for an easier and simpler way to establish property rights and calculate property tax. It involves:

- making a complete aerial survey of Costa Rica;

- reforming all laws pertaining to real estate;

- creating national policy for resolving property disputes;

- modernizing with computerized data collection in all 81 local authorities that handle property taxes, to create a unified property record for the whole country.

Once the transfer title has been presented to the Public Registry upon closing, you have three-months' protection should an unscrupulous seller try to sell the property again. If your title is presented after three months, a subsequent deed could have priority and you could lose your land.

Using the premise of *first in time, first in right*, priority is given based on the date the title is recorded. Whoever presents the transfer (*anotación*) first to the Registry is recorded as the legal owner even though they might have 'bought' the property after you did. As you can see, it is imperative to get your property presented and registered in the Registry as soon as possible after closing.

Even if you present your deed in time, it also must be registered within one year or it will be cancelled by the Registry.

> Unlike many foreign countries, **you do not have to be a legal resident** of Costa Rica to own property here. You can own property in your own name or a corporate name.

Five Easy Steps To Do Your Own Simple Title Search Of A Costa Rican Property Online In Your Own Home!

The bad news is that the Website we are about to show you is 100% Spanish; however, the good news is that even if all you can only say, "*Dos cervezas, por favor!*" ("Two beers, please."), with this handy guide, **in under five minutes**, you will find what you want.

Please make sure you have the six-digit title number (*folio real*) of the property that you wish to check:

- Visit **registronacional.go.cr** – This site can sometimes be busy so please be patient.

- On the top menu bar, click on the word *Consultas.*

- At the next menu, click on *Bienes Inmuebles.* On the right side of your screen, click on *Por Número de Finca o Concesión.*

- At the next menu, make sure you insert the correct *Provincia* and where it says *Finca*, type in the title number (*folio real*) of the property and then hit *Consultar.*

Then right before your very eyes, you will see the property owner's name (*proprietario*).

On this screen, you will clearly see a description of the property and the size (*mide*). For example it may say "*MIL OCHOCIENTOS SETENTA Y SEIS METROS CUADRADOS*" which would be 1,876 m2 (20,185 ft2).

The most important information we're looking for is on the bottom half of the screen:

- **Who exactly** is the legal owner (*proprietario*) of the property.

- **Any legal complications** or more accurately, encumbrances.

The owner's name is clearly listed under the word *Proprietario.* The line below gives you the owner's identification number (*cédula de identidad*) and then his/her marital status.

At the very bottom of this page, you want to see the following words *Gravamenes: "NO HAY"*, meaning that there are no obligations or encumbrances.

If there are *Gravemenes* listed, this is the time to speak to your attorney who will do a more in-depth title search to help you understand exactly what those problems might be. They could be minor and easy to resolve; on the other hand, they may not be.

You can also see the history of that property by clicking on *Historia*.

Please note that after you have bought real estate in Costa Rica, for your own peace of mind, **it is extremely important** you verify your ownership has indeed been recorded at **registronacional.go.cr**

Now you know how you can easily do this yourself following the simple steps above. Within 45 days, you should see that you are the new owner and if you cannot, consult with your attorney and see why there is a delay.

Are you hoping to build a *Cadillac* styled home on a *Budweiser* budget? You can learn more by reading our articles at **WeLoveCostaRica.com**

How To Ensure The Car You Want To Buy Is Owned By The Person Who Is Trying To Sell It To You

If you are planning on buying a car in Costa Rica, the very same **registronacional.go.cr** Website will list the owner of any car registered in Costa Rica. And yes! There have been cases where a trusting buyer has bought a car only to discover later that the car was sold by someone other than the real owner of the car. As always, you do need to do your homework and as you now know, it's simple, very easy and should not take more than five minutes.

Simply follow the easy steps below to see car's current owner listed:

1. Visit **registronacional.go.cr**

2. On the top menu bar, click on the word *Consultas*.

3. At the next menu, click on *Bienes Muebles*. (Please note this is different from the earlier instructions on property checks above – *Muebles* and not *Inmuebles*) On the right hand side of your screen, click on *Vehiculos*.

4. At the next menu, click on *Placa* and insert the plate number of the car you wish to buy and then hit *Consultar*.

5. Then right before your very eyes, you will see the correct legal owner of the car. You might also want to click on *Infracciones* to see if there have been any problems with the car. After you have clicked on that, you want to see the words *Vehiculo no tiene Infracciones*.

Real Estate Attorneys

Fine, back home, your specialized real estate or conveyance attorney charges a nice big fee and comes up with the goods. The paperwork is put in order, you are protected against any possible problems and hindrances that might prevent a satisfactory closing of the purchase and you walk away happy as the 'king of your new castle'.

Will that happen in Costa Rica? Not necessarily! Firstly, **the law in Costa Rica is different**.

Costa Rica applies Napoleonic or Civil Law, unlike the Common Law in the US, Canada and much of Europe. Most of the complaints heard from frustrated foreigners are that their notaries or lawyers were inefficient, didn't protect their interests aggressively enough, didn't follow through with details and as for communications – forget it!

If your lawyer does find a problem, **he may not want to share it with you** - in typical *Tico* fashion that avoids confrontation, he may stick his head in the proverbial sand and hope the problem will go away or that you won't ask about it.

Are you looking for reliable, trustworthy, experienced, reference-checked real estate professionals in Costa Rica? Please visit **WeLoveCostaRica.com** and click on '**Help-U-Search**'.

So **what should your attorney do** for you during the purchase process?

He will check over all the documentation from the purchase agreement to the transfer of title and advise you if there are irregularities.

He will verify that the person selling is the legal owner of the property through the *Registro Nacional*, if an individual owner. This you can also do yourself. If the property is owned by a corporation, he will check through the Commercial Section (*Sección Mercántil*) of the *Registro*, that **the person selling is part of that corporation** and is the legal signatory able to sign on behalf of the corporation.

The *Registro* provides much information about the property and any liens and annotations, but it does not necessarily give all the details (restrictions for future roads or zoning restrictions or underground water rights of access). These can only be found out with a **full title search.**

The expanded title search is done at the local municipal authority (*Municipio*) and can mean digging through the older paper records for any taxes, zoning regulations, easements and liens that did not show up in the *Registro*. Not all data is recorded electronically and some older properties demand hours spent going through dusty files.

Depending on your country of residence, owning your Costa Rica home in the name of a corporation may also have tax benefits back home.

Your attorney should help with payment transactions and make sure your down payment and other payments are protected.

He can place an annotation on the property that you want, which will *hold* it for three months. This stops the property from being registered by someone else should the vendor try to sell it twice over.

What you must establish with your attorney:

- **Tell him you expect him to do** all the above!

- **Establish his fee** for closing. The fees you pay your attorney can be based on a fixed amount, a percentage of the purchase price of the property (usually 1.25% of the purchase price), an hourly rate or a combination. It is in your own interests to have this clearly established before going too far and have an agreement put in writing to avoid misunderstandings later on.

- You need to understand and be happy with the documentation, especially if you are going to be signing it. Don't put up with impatience or being rushed.

- **Get certified copies of everything!** File them, keep them, do not lose them!

Hoping to buy land first and build on it later? You can see what you have to be careful of by reading our articles at
WeLoveCostaRica.com

How To Check Up On Costa Rican Attorneys

Do you know if there have been any major complaints filed against the Costa Rican attorney that you are dealing with? Would you **prefer to be sure?**

Even if your Spanish is bad, you can easily find this information yourself at the *Colegio de Abogados de Costa Rica* Website (www.abogados.or.cr) and then click on *Quejas y Suspensiones* (Complaints & Suspensions).

Here you will find details of all the attorneys that have had **serious disciplinary problems.** For example, you will find attorneys listed as suspended for disciplinary causes or *Causas Disciplinarias*. As you will see, some have more than one suspension.

You will also find attorneys suspended for tardiness or delays (*Suspendidos por Morosidad*) meaning they probably did not submit legal papers on time etc. This is NOT as serious as the suspensions above but we all want to work with attorneys that are qualified, honest and efficient, right?

If you need help in finding good, bilingual attorneys to help you with your Costa Rica real estate transactions, please visit **WeLoveCostaRica.com** then Contact Us and we'll be happy to recommend someone to you.

The Public Notary

The public notary is a key figure in the purchase process and wields a lot of power! **All Costa Rica notaries are also attorneys** although **not all attorneys are public notaries** so you could theoretically get a notary to act as your real estate attorney as well.

However, both parties (seller and buyer) must agree upon who the public notary is to be for closing the transfer and registering the deeds.

Since the notary has to be impartial, it isn't always practical that he/she be your legal representative as well. Conversely, be careful that if the notary is chosen by the seller, your interests will also be provided for, especially when it comes to the vital step of registering the deeds with the *Registro.*

The rule of thumb about finding a notary is:

- if you are paying the full purchase price upon closing, **you get to choose** the public notary;

- if the seller is helping you to finance your purchase, **he gets to choose**;

- if you have a bank loan or mortgage to cover the purchase, **the bank will want to choose**;

- if neither side can agree about notaries, then each can choose their own and the two joint notaries are used for the closing deeds transfer. It's more costly but it stops the squabbling!

If you get to choose the notary, and you decide to use your attorney, then he will benefit from these notary fees as well as his legal fees.

Please show some compassion when you see the driver in front of you weaving all over the road; he's probably not drunk, he's just trying to avoid all the potholes.

What else does or should the public notary do before executing the deeds? He can go over pretty much the same check-list of required steps your real estate attorney should have completed during the purchase process. It seems like unnecessary duplication, but if you and your attorney have already taken the steps to your satisfaction, the public notary's search only helps confirm that everything is in order. To reiterate, the notary will:

- check the property in the *Registro* for any **liens or encumbrances** or registered conditions that might have been overlooked by the buyer;

- advise you if there are any liens or restrictions, so they are stated in the deeds with your consent;

- make sure the property is **registered in the owner's name** and that person has the right to transfer title to you;

- will draft the transfer deeds. The document is put into the notary's protocol book (*protocolo*), the register of all public documents issued by that notary.

Once signed, he is responsible for annotating and registering the deeds in the *Registro* as soon as possible. To do this, all relevant documentation must be attached and in order and his fees paid.

The list below gives the relevant documentation, taxes and fees due before registration can take place.

- **Land taxes**. Proof of full payment by seller (*constancia municipal sobre impuesto de bienes inmuebles*).
- **Municipal taxes**. Proof of full payment by seller (*constancia municipal*).
- Payment of all **transaction fees** and taxes - provided by both sides.
- Payment of **notary fees** - provided by both sides.
- Copy of **survey map** with map number.
- Authorization if the land is to be split from an original property.
- Powers of attorney if necessary.

This list may change over time or be amended so check with your attorney and notary before closing.

If the notary does not have these documents or payments, he is not obliged to finalize the registration of your deeds. He is, however, still responsible for presenting the deeds to the *Registro* for annotation.

This protects you as the buyer so that nobody else can present subsequent documents that could affect your rights of ownership. That is why it is so important you make sure the notary immediately presents the deeds once signed. It is also important that the deeds are registered within one year after execution so they are not annulled.

If, once the notary has drafted the deeds for execution and you do not go through with closing, you must pay a **penalty fee of 25%** of the notary's full due fees.

Any claims against a Public Notary are filed through the National Notary Office (*Dirección Nacional de Notariado*).

You can hire a full-time maid in Costa Rica for about US$250 per month. My maid Lily comes in for two hours per day, five days per week and she receives about US$20 for the week.

The Notary's Fees

The fees you pay the notary cover the notarization, drafting, drawing up, annotation and registration of the final deeds. The fees are fixed at 1.5% for the first one million colones, and 1.25% for the remainder of the purchase price.

Closing Costs

It is customary for **buyer and seller to share the closing costs** equally unless otherwise agreed.

Before the transfer deed can be placed into the Registry, all transfer taxes, stamps, notary fees, mortgage costs (if applicable) and property taxes must be paid. The Public Registry will not record a transfer deed unless everything has been fully paid. You have already seen that notary fees are set at 1.5 - 1.25%.

Property **transfer** tax (*Impuesto de Traspaso*) comes to 1.5% of the registered value of the property so **expect to pay 3.4%** of your total declared transfer purchase price to complete the transfer.

You also have to pay stamp duty. The government requires that documentary stamps be affixed to the deed. These stamps include the following: Municipal Stamp: (*Timbre Municipal*); Legal Bar Association Stamp (*Timbre del Colegio de Abogados*); Agricultural Stamp (*Timbre Agrario*); National Archives Stamp (*Timbre del Archivo Nacional*); Fiscal Stamp: (*Especie Fiscal*).

The Public Registry also imposes its own tax of .05% on presented documents to be recorded in the Public Registry (*Derechos de Registro*). As you can see, your deeds are well decorated with stamps by the time they reach the filing cabinet!

Do you plan on starting your own business in Costa Rica? Would a report called *21 Tips to Starting Your Own Business in Costa Rica* help you? You can learn more by visiting the Costa Rica Business section of **WeLoveCostaRica.com**

Estimate of Closing Costs on US$100K Property
(Using exchange rate of 455 colones: US$1

1. Purchase price:

Valor de Venta (Sales Price)	US$100,000
Valor Registral (Registered Price)	US$100,000

2. Transfer Taxes & Stamps:

a. Property Transfer Tax 1.5%	US$1,500 (Ley 7293-7543)
b. National Public Registry Fee 0.05%	US$500 (Ley 6575)
c. Documentary Stamps	
c(i). Municipal Stamp 0.2%	US$200 (Ley 6890)
c(ii). Fiscal Ley 7535 0.2%	US$215 (Ley 7535)
c(iii). Agrarian Stamp 0.1%	US$100 (Ley 5792-6735)
c(iv). Bar Association Stamp	US$1.98 (Decree 20307-J)
c(v). National Archives Stamp	US$0.04 (Ley 7202)
c(vi). Fiscal	US$1.38

Sub Total Closing Costs   US$2,518.40

3. Notary Fee

1.5% of first million colones   US$32.97 (Decree 20307-J)
1.25% of remaining purchase price   US$1,222.53 (21365-J/22308-J)

Sub Total Notary Fee   US$1,255.49

Total Closing Costs   **US$3,773.89**

Total Paid by Seller (50%)   US$1,886.95
Total Paid by Buyer (50%)   US$1,886.95

Mortgage costs. It is customary for the person receiving financing to pay the costs of drafting and registering the mortgage. A mortgage can be created at the same time as the sale by adding a mortgage clause in the transfer deed, or a separate mortgage can be drafted.

The public notary will charge for drawing up the mortgage document and that fee can range from approximately 0.625% to 1.25% of the amount of the mortgage, depending on the circumstances involved.

The buyer should be aware that Costa Rican real estate transactions commonly operate on a two-tiered system. In general terms, Costa Rican properties have a low property tax appraisal base in relation to market value; as such, it has become a customary practice to run property sales through at the registered value, which may be substantially less than the actual sales price of the property.

In such a case, all transfer taxes and fees discussed above would apply to the registered value as opposed to its sales price, with the exception of the notary fee. Buyers should consult their attorney about the potential risks of this practice. (See Manipulating the Declared Transfer Price below.)

Translation costs. If you require the deeds to be translated for you to fully understand them, this must be factored in at this stage.

The bad news is we do have tollbooths in Costa Rica. The good news is that they are typically only 75 colones which is about US$0.16 cents and in rush hour they open up the gates and let you drive through for free. Go figure!

Other Costs During the Purchase Process

- Broker's commission (usually paid by seller) 5 - 10%.

- Attorney's fees.

- Additional topography fees or other appraisals or searches.

- Title Insurance, around 1.5%.

- Surveyor or engineer's reports to inspect buildings.

- Escrow fees if payment needs to be put in escrow.

Basically, you can factor in **an extra 7 - 15% on top of the purchase price** to cover all additional costs.

Manipulating The Declared Transfer Price

It has been common practice to declare a lower purchase price than the actual amount paid by buyer to seller to avoid paying the full whack for the various transfer taxes and stamps and to reduce the notary's fees. It also reduces annual land taxes based on the registered purchase price.

This constitutes tax fraud and is considered a felony. Modernized data information systems in the municipal offices keep closer controls on property values and if they suspect your property is undervalued, they will re-evaluate it according to current market prices for that area. You could end up paying extra taxes and the notary could legally collect an adjusted fee based on the amended value.

United States citizens can own foreign real estate in their IRA and 401(k). The Roth IRA is an ideal vehicle for those who are eligible. The rules governing buying real estate in an IRA and 401(k) are strict so get professional advice.

Title Guaranty

Since real estate titles are publicly registered, you can make use of a title guaranty from a title insurance company protecting the buyer by guaranteeing the property is free of any liens and other impediments that could hinder the purchase process and/or restrict your full rights as owner.

A title guaranty can help protect you against:

- false identity of the person selling;

- invalid, or out-of-date falsified documentation;

- liens or encumbrances pertaining to the previous owner;

- hidden heirs or anything else that could affect your purchase.

A title insurance company helps protects your interests as a buyer and can offer a range of products to help throughout the entire transaction. It depends on your level of confidence in your broker, your ability to complete the transaction in a foreign country and your trust in your attorney.
Some services that may be offered are:

- Trust. The company investigates the property to guarantee that the person selling is the rightful, legal owner.

- Title Guaranty. This protects you against any title defects, liens or other hurdles that could prevent you from closing on the property of your choice.

- Escrow. If, as is usual here, the seller wants a deposit from you to show good faith in your intention to buy the property, the deposit can be placed in escrow with an impartial third-party service. This avoids any mis-handling of funds, ensures the funds are safe and protects against fraud.

- Future Guaranty. The moment of final transfer of the deeds is a stressful time. This protects against possible fraudulent transfers or hidden heirs and will provide full compensation and legal recourse in the event that a fraudulent transfer has taken place.

As with any other contract, find out what you are covered for and carefully check all the terms and conditions in the small print.

Unscrupulous brokers don't like me saying this but … unless you are convinced Costa Rica is where you want to live, don't rush to move here. Visit numerous times in different months (including the rainy season) before you finally decide to put your money down and buy a property.

If you would like more detailed information about how title guaranty could help protect you with your real estate purchase in Costa Rica, please visit **WeLoveCostaRica.com** and then click on Contact Us.

Property Taxes

As an owner, whether of a building or land, **you must pay annual property taxes** to your local municipal authority according to the value assigned to the lot . This taxable amount has to be re-evaluated every five years. Costa Rica Property Law calculates the charges according to each municipal area but, strange as it may seem, you are responsible for providing the re-evaluation.

Costa Rica property taxes are charged annually as ¢2,500 for each million colones, depending on the calculated taxable value of the property.

So for example, if your property has a calculated taxable value of US$250,000 then your property taxes will be US$625 per year (0.25%) which makes Costa Rica an **extremely affordable** place to own real estate.

The value is declared by anyone in possession of land, not necessarily the owner. There are two key valuation parameters to calculate the taxable value of the property. These are known as the *Plano de Valores* (Valuation Table) and the *Tipología Constructiva* (Building Characteristics), both under the Tax Office's Technical Standardization Department.

The Valuation Table is a tool that helps calculate the taxable value per square meter according to the zone where the property is located, be that a building plot or construction. The physical characteristics of the land are calculated: is it a corner or middle site, is it in a commercial, residential or industrial zone, does it have full services (sewage, electricity, telephone, etc.), what topographical features affect the property. These are compared with other lots within the same zone. The zones are determined by the Technical Norms Department of the Tax Office and they are published in the official government news sheet *La Gaceta*. Another important consideration is the property's saleable value.

Look for great schools (even if you don't have children) as they are often in the fastest-appreciating neighborhoods. (But remember that this doesn't necessarily mean your children can get into that great school.)

The Building Characteristics are defined by the materials used and the design of the building and takes their depreciation into account. Parameters used are area, type of outside walls, floors, ceilings, roofs, number of rooms and bathrooms, age of construction and any remodeling. Something to note is that the **square-meter value of a building is the same throughout the country for tax purposes** whereas the square-meter value for land varies according to its zoning.

The sum of both calculations less depreciation adds up to the property's taxable value. A description of the land and its value are presented to calculate the tax. If the calculation of the estimated value looks suspiciously low, the Administrative Tax Department will come along to appraise the value and it can turn out to be much higher than the one the landholder considers to be fair and just.

Should the tax-paying owner not agree with the taxable value placed on his property, a claim can be made to the tax department of the local courts, the local municipal authority, the central administrative Tax Office or in the open courts.

It is possible to apply for tax exoneration but this is normally only granted when the property owner, as an individual, registers a single property in the National Registry. Once the amount is fixed for the five-year period, it can be divided into four quarterly payments. The payable amount is one quarter of a percent of the land value as registered in the Tax Office.

When you close on your land purchase, a certified copy of the deeds must be sent to the local municipal authority within one month to update the register.

Want to see how a US businessman runs a successful multi-million-dollar business in the US while enjoying life in Costa Rica? You can learn more by reading our articles at **WeLoveCostaRica.com**

Chapter Six

Financing Your Purchase

One thing that can be forgotten in the heat of all this house buying is how exactly are you going to pay for it? No, not whether you have the cash or savings or inheritance but how do you physically send your money to the seller. US-based cashier's checks can take weeks to clear and you could lose your dream home to other interested parties simply because it takes a while to get the money here.

Once you decide you are going to buy in Costa Rica, go to one of the reputable banks, open a dollar account, which can take some time depending on your nationality and country of residence, transfer your funds and then you can issue a cashier's check here that is immediately redeemable. This is how most property transactions are done – with a cashier's check or wire transfer.

A seller may be prepared to help finance a buyer and legal measures are in place to accommodate this option. However, if you want to go down the mortgage route, be advised that although this seems a feasible alternative, you will need to be totally clear what is being offered and what the conditions of repayment are.

Mortgages

Several banks in Costa Rica offer mortgages.

If you seriously think this is worthwhile, then **be prepared for a mountain of paperwork** and plenty of time allocated as communications swing back and forth between your original country and Costa Rica.

The loan amount is not necessarily based on the sale price established between you as buyer and the seller. The bank's appraiser will survey the house and, based on that assessment, you can expect to receive a loan worth a maximum of 70% of the appraised value of whichever is lower between the sale price and the appraisal.

If internet access is important to you, remember that not all areas have internet cable access. If your business depends on the internet, you must be in an area that has internet cable service. Most people become frustrated trying to use the telephone connection for emails and internet.

Documents You Will Need To Produce:

- Signed application form;

- Social Security number;

- Evidence of your last address in the US;

- Copies of tax returns for the past three years;

- An income certification made by a CPA (Certified Public Accountant) indicating monthly gross income (issued in Costa Rica) or by the Costa Rica Consul in the US or the Costa Rica Consul in your country of origin;

- A copy of bank statements of current, savings, investments and/or retirement accounts for previous six months;

- Copy of last payment made for mortgage or other loans;

- Copies of the last six months of credit card statements. The bank carries out credit searches in your previous country of residence. All credit accounts must be presented to the bank;

- A copy of two ID cards with photos (drivers license, passport);

- Copies of utility bills in Costa Rica;

- Evidence of assets (deed of warranties, certificates of title) either in your name or that of your corporation;

- Other assets such as vehicles and properties;

- Proof that all municipal taxes have been paid for the property in question;

- A copy of purchase option agreement and down-payment receipt;

- Two registered copies of the survey plans (*catastro nacional*);

- If you are applying for a loan for building, you must also present:
    - o The building plans approved by the *Colegio de Ingenieros y Arquitectos* and the relevant municipal authority;
    - o Building schedule;

o   Outline of the construction budget.

- If you are applying for a loan for refinancing purposes, you must present:

    o   Last letter or receipt from the creditor;
    o   Other documentation as stipulated by the bank if the property is in the name of a corporation.

Ask about power-cuts (brownouts) and water shortages. There are a few problem areas so make sure you ask specifically about these kinds of problems in the areas where you are considering living. If you don't ask, you will probably not be told about them.

Income must be verified according to the following categories. If you are a:

- **salaried borrower** working for a company registered in Costa Rica, you must present an **income verification letter** issued by the company and addressed specifically to the bank. The letter must indicate the length of time you have worked for the company, job position, and gross and net salary. Include the *orden patron*al, the official registration of an employee with the Costa Rica Social Security Department (*Caja Costariccense de Seguro Social*), which lists the salary paid by the employer to the employee.

- **self-employed borrower**, you must produce a **certified copy of your income** by an authorized CPA registered in Costa Rica, specifically addressed to the bank indicating your company's activity, current job position, average gross and net income during the last fiscal period and an up-to-date average. It must include mention of all resources used to certify income such as account statements, receipts, etc.

- **borrower with foreign income**, you must produce a **certified copy of income** by an authorized CPA approved of by that bank, registered in Costa Rica, specifically addressed to the bank, indicating the company's activity, current job position, average gross and net income during last fiscal period and an up-to-date average. It must include mention of all resources used to certify income such as account statements, receipts.

Some sellers (not just *Ticos*) will ask for outrageous, insanely high prices for their homes and European, Canadian or American *logic* will not necessarily work when you make what you think is a reasonable offer. You can sometimes negotiate truly terrific deals but this obviously depends on the personalities involved and the financial needs of the seller.

What the Banks Are Offering

Most mortgages fall into categories for ready-built properties with or without existing mortgages, land to be constructed and improvements, repairs and/or extensions to existing property.

Interest rates change and these quoted are good as at February, 2005:

Banco San José offers a 15 – 20 year mortgage on a minimum of US$30K to maximum of $400K. For loans up to $150K, financing up to 80%; over $150K financing is 70%. From $300K to $400K, it drops to 60%. For repairs, improvements and extensions, financing based on 70% of a loan worth $30K to $300K. Charges are 5.5% over the 3-month Libor rate with a ceiling of 7%.

LAFISE offers dollar financing with a fixed rate of 9.5% for 15 – 17-year loans on a maximum of $350K. Bank charges and legal fees are around 8%. Credit lines of 10, 12 and 15 years are also offered at a 7.5% variable rate.

Scotiabank offers dollar or colon loans with 15- to 30-year options; interest rates dependent on currency, and even a *ScotiaMix* of both currencies to suit client needs of up to 85% of the total value of the property. Interest rates are variable at between 20 – 21.5% in colones and 7.5 – 9.75% in US dollars depending on repayment schedules. Bank fees and processing charges are around 6.32% for colones, 7.5% for dollars.

Interfin offers loans in colones on a basic borrowing rate plus 1% for the first year up to 5% for the third, financing to a maximum of 80% of the assessed value up from 13 million to a maximum of 22 million colones at 15 to 20 years. Debt-to-income ratio is a maximum 30%.

Cuscatlán offers both dollar and colon credit up to a maximum 20-year term for financing between $30K to $250K. Based on a $100K loan, bank charges, commission and legal fees run at around 8.478%.

Banex also offers loans in dollars and colones. The dollar credit interest rate is Libor plus 5.5% up to 25 years with a minimum of $35K, in colones it the base rate plus 5.5% over 30 years for a minimum 10 million colones. Both incur bank charges of around 5.8%

Property Protection

There are **two ways to protect your property** from being fraudulently transferred.

1. You can file a voluntary request to the National Registry (*Registro Nacional*) asking them to **freeze your title** (*Inmovilizacion de Finca por Limites Voluntarios*). This prohibits any National Registry employee from recording any transfer document filed against the property. If you decide to sell the property, you will have to first go through the process of removing this restriction.

2. Another common way to make your property less appealing is by **having a lien on your property** in the form of a mortgage bond (*cédulas hipotecárias*). The property owner requests, by way of a public notary that mortgage bonds be issued against titled property for an amount established by the property owner. The National Registry places an annotation on the property and issues the mortgage bonds which are physically delivered to the property owner.

This mechanism is used in commerce whereby property owners pledge the certificate bonds for cash or offer them as collateral on other loans. When the loan or pledge is paid off, the lender returns the bonds to the property owner who can continue to reuse them in the same manner.

Since the bonds are an encumbrance on the property it is less appealing for those intending to depose you of your property since they would have to contend with the encumbrance.

The costs of creating mortgage bonds on the property is comparable to the cost of forming a normal mortgage, less than 1.3% of the property value with the bulk of the expense going to the notary fee.

A mortgage bond is an effective legal mechanism to protect your real estate assets but if you would like to explore this further, please make sure you hire an experienced notary who knows how to register mortgage certificates (*cédulas hipotecárias*); many notaries know nothing about them.

As always, if you would like a proven recommendation of someone that can help you protect your property, please visit **WeLoveCostaRica.com** and then click on Contact Us.

You can practically **choose your own weather** in Costa Rica (except snow). It varies from hot coastal lowlands to cool mountainous regions. The average temperature in the Central Valley is ideal with evenings of 17-18 C and days averaging 25-28°C (77-82.°F) year round. The dry season is usually from the end of November until after Easter.

Using Your Retirement Accounts To Buy Property

What Are Your Options?

Did you know that you can invest in real estate, in the US as well as many other countries related to mortgages, leases, and other asset-backed investments? Costa Rica is no exception.

Recent articles in *The Wall Street Journal, Time, MSN* and *AARP* publications have brought the practice of retirement self-direction into the public's awareness. It has proven to be a powerful vehicle to build investment wealth while reducing, or eliminating, future tax considerations; yet historically, it has generally only been the high-net-worth individuals that have availed themselves of this opportunity.

Surprising to some, self-directed plans have been available since 1975, although relatively few IRA holders have taken the time to understand their options and take advantage of such plans. Recently, the IRS has increased the contribution limits to unprecedented levels for most plans. For example, business owners without common law employees may qualify for the Individual or Solo plan and thus defer up to 100% of their first $14,000 and up to $42,000 annually.

There are three things you should know when you self-direct your retirement plan:

1. Which retirement plans are best: Traditional IRA, Roth IRA, SEP, Simple or Individual?

2. What types of investments you want to make within the plan?

3. The IRS rules of self-dealing and prohibited transactions.

The IRS rules regarding prohibited transactions are not too complex, yet one should consult a tax advisor for specific advice. Disqualified people include your immediate family (except siblings) employers (in a qualified plan), certain partners, fiduciaries and other categories spelled out in IRS code.

IRA owners may not borrow money from their IRA, sell property to it, receive unreasonable compensation for managing it, or use as security for a loan.

There are also several named categories, such a collectables which also may not be held by your IRA.

The opportunities outside these prohibited transactions are significant. You may buy, sell or exchange investment property. You can partner with friends, relatives and business associates to purchase property, then lease it to anyone that is not a disqualified person. You can roll property from one plan to another - or even take property from your plan as a distribution.

We have seen clients form investment groups, combining IRA and non-IRA funds to purchase and hold property, rehab and turn properties or simply lend out the funds in the form of notes and mortgages.

In addition to these ideas, an IRA may also invest in partnerships, LLCs, private stock offerings, loans (both secured and unsecured), tax lien certificates, purchase options, joint ventures and other investments.

So if you are confident in your abilities to make your own investment decisions, have the desire to reduce or eliminate the tax consequences on your gains, and have the resources to invest, self-direction may prove to be a wise choice.

Our thanks to Glen Mather of Entrust Administration Services, which has offices in Orlando and Miami providing self-directed administration for clients in 24 states, Canada and the Virgin Islands.

Steps For Purchasing Property In Your IRA

- **Draw up a purchase agreement** naming your IRA as legal owner once you find the property you want;

- Arrange to pay the deposit out of your IRA with your administrator. If this looks like it will take too long and you have ready cash, you can pay this first yourself and be reimbursed by the IRA administrator, or have it wire-transferred directly;

- Send a Buy Direction Letter to the administrator outlining your instructions for purchasing the real estate;

- Have the real estate attorney, the escrow company and all other people involved in the transaction contact the IRA administrator: He/she will advise you of the necessary forms needed to close the deal. Once completed and returned to the administrator by all concerned, a copy of the contract should also be sent;

- All documentation should be sent to the administrator who signs on your IRA's behalf. He will check them against the information you sent initially in your Buy Direction Letter and sign the documents;

- A replacement check or wire transfer to replace the deposit payment is sent to pay the seller or seller's attorney;

- The administrator arranges a wire transfer into the escrow account to buy the property;

- Since you cannot collect any income from the property if it is intended as an income-generating property, contract a reputable property management company for this purpose;

- Any profits are now cash in your IRA and can be invested accordingly as instructed in your Buy Direction Letter.

According to Richard Philps, an experienced Canadian attorney living and working in Costa Rica, "Canadian investors with self-directed RRSP portfolios are able to invest up to 30% of the value of their portfolio in **foreign investments not involving real property**. Such investments must be *arms-length* transactions such as stocks or bonds issued by corporate or business entities in which the investor does not have a personal interest."

If you are Canadian and would like to speak to Richard Philps – a Canadian attorney who will soon be a fully qualified Costa Rican attorney, please visit **WeLoveCostaRica.com** and click on Contact Us.

Real Estate Investment Trusts

One way to invest in real estate is to invest in a publicly traded Costa Rica REIT. Available to US and Canadian citizens, it is an easy-to-follow option and some trusts offer diversification benefits based as geography and property types. Unfortunately, the Costa Rica REITs tend to have some **outrageously high annual management fees.**

What are they exactly? REITS are publicly held funds that buy and hold different kinds of property and generate income from renting the properties to companies or individuals. Investors buy shares entitling them to part of the fund's assets as well as dividends. Normally, new buildings are bought in booming areas although older or historically interesting buildings have been targeted for this kind of investment.

When parking your car on the street or near a strip mall, there is often an 'unofficial' guard there who will guide you in and out of a parking space and watch your car for you. Known as a *watchingman*, he should be tipped about 200 colones (50 cents) for stays of more than half an hour. Whether he actually 'guards' your car is another matter…

Chapter Seven

Buying Ready Made

We have continually emphasized that whether you are going to buy an existing house or build your own, you need to be informed. This applies when you are choosing your broker and your attorney. It also applies to the search on any property that interests you. It means finding out the best deals should you consider trying to take out a real estate loan from a bank (See Section on **Mortgages**).

Housing Options

Once upon a time, Costa Rica meant living on the land and from the land. Houses were either simple adobe homes nestling in their own gardens or fields, small or large town houses that stepped out directly onto the street or grand plantation mansions set in their own grounds.

Now, with foreign-influenced architectural and residential designs, it's up to you what design you go for. Let's look at some of the main categories of ready-made residential options:

> Why do sophisticated investors feel safer banking in Switzerland than in Costa Rica? Visit **WeLoveCostaRica.com** and then click on Contact Us.

Independent, Stand-Alone Housing

The simple *Tico* country single-storey houses are still abundant on the market, as well as comfortable independent town houses. These are located in the older, established districts such as Moravia, Los Yoses and Rohrmoser or the country towns of Santa Ana, Ciudad Colón and in the outer reaches of the Central Valley, such as Atenas and La Garita or Cartago and Tres Rios.

If you are looking in the Golden Triangle, you will find large American-style mansions set in their own grounds with efficient security systems, but much new construction is being centered around condominiums and gated community estates.

Condominiums

Condo living is nothing new to Americans and the advantages are obvious for foreigners who commute between Costa Rica and other countries during the year.

There are two main kinds of condo (*Propiedad en Condominio*): private condominium development, or a unit within a full-amenity resort-style compound. Both offer **security**. You can shut the place down, lock the door and leave, knowing your home is safe.

Potential downsides are living so close to the neighbors who might be noisy or have barking dogs, **which is a common problem**, and you have to abide by certain condominium regulations that might not suit your independent outlook.

You need to be aware of specific condo laws when you buy into a condominium. Condominiums must be registered in the Public Registry (*Registro Nacional de la Propiedad*). This provides it with a similar structure to a company with a governing body and administrator.

Condominiums are built on a *finca madre* or common ground that is jointly owned by all condo owners. The *finca filiales* are the individually owned units on that common ground within the condominium.

The condo can have a bank account, sign contracts and appear in court. Article #28 states that the condominium association must log all resolutions in a minutes book. It must also provide an accounting to its association members on a yearly basis.

A property owners' association must be formed that will prepare a *reglamento* or bylaws including:

- an elected administrator;

- what each owner must pay in maintenance fees;

- the frequency of General Assembly meetings;

- an outline of the rights and use of the common grounds;

- an outline for solving disputes and sanctions between neighbors;

- regulations for the decoration and styles allowed on facades.

> If you get angry and frustrated every time you have to reset the digital clock again on your microwave and stereo, Costa Rica will probably not be the right place for you. We do get power-cuts.

Gated Communities

These have become increasingly popular with wealthier *Ticos*, Americans and Europeans because they combine security with lots of shared extras. At the top end of the range, you will find resort-style communities with full-scale sports and residential facilities.

Three main types of gated developments are available in Costa Rica:

Resort-style gated communities. Resort communities with full amenities are still a new concept here. Typically, they are high-density residential areas fronted by an international flagship hotel chain and offer full sports facilities, private club for owners, restaurants, marinas and shopping outlets.

Currently, the only resorts of this kind are the Los Sueños Resort & Marina anchored by the Marriot Hotel and the Conchal Resort by Melia. The huge three-phase Peninsula Papagayo project will offer hotels, golf courses, marina, pools and commercial outlets; this gives some indication of trends and is by far the most ambitious resort-community project seen so far in Costa Rica (see the **What's Where** section).

Gated Community (1/4- to two-acre plots). High-density, strictly regulated resort estates are not to everyone's taste. Many buyers want the security and amenities of a private community but also the independence to design their own homes with fewer units in the master plan. These communities offer a property owners' association to determine issues of common interest to the residents.

Gated Large-Plot Community (three to ten acres). If you want the feel of being surrounded by your own piece of forest or at least have the impression you are almost king of all you survey, a few gated communities offer large plots that still combine the security of controlled access with some shared amenities.

> Interested in **Tax Saving Tips for US Expats**? You can learn more by reading our articles at **WeLoveCostaRica.com**

The Central Valley and elsewhere in the southern Pacific zone have seen many smaller gated communities popping up with houses set into spacious lots from 1/4 to three acres.

You will have a common social area with pool and barbecue facilities and 24/7 guard service. Prices vary tremendously with houses in these communities going from as little as US$55K to over US$1 million.

If you would like more detailed information about these kinds of developments, please visit **www.WeLoveCostaRica.com** and then click on Contact Us.

Apartment Blocks

Custom-built apartment blocks are relatively new on the Costa Rica scene but they are appearing with the demand for secure, quality, easy-maintenance housing alternatives near San José and its amenities and don't cost a fortune.

Urban-centered apartments are useful if you work downtown and don't want to commute for hours struggling with clogged Central Valley traffic or if being near city amenities is important to you. Sometimes the difference from condos is a bit confusing and basically they both require a property owners' association and bylaws; you will have to pay community and maintenance fees for both. Essentially, apartment blocks are just that – single or multiple units per floor with some common social areas.

Condos can include town-house styles of two-storey terraced houses or even independent villas within a secure compound with often a greater range of shared amenities. The almost completed *Brisas del Oeste* apartment project a couple of kilometers west of downtown San José, incorporating 160 apartments in four towers is a fairly new concept in Costa Rica.

Located just west of Sabana Park, it hopes to combine ease of access into the city centre with good road access to Escazú and the airport. It also offers on-site shopping, safe covered parking and 24/7 security with **starting prices around US$75K** for a two-bedroom quality apartment. This could well be the trend in urban housing in coming years.

Costa Ricans have more names. Marisol María Brenes Chavarria means that Marisol is her first name. María is her second name (like our middle name). Brenes is the surname of her father and Chavarria the mother's maiden name. Should she marry, say, Juan Castro, she becomes Marisol Maria Brenes Castro!

Income-Generating Properties

Buying a house is **a substantial investment** so you don't want to lose money on it. One idea is to make your property work for you.

Time Share. If you don't intend living in Costa Rica year-round, you can buy into a resort community - a bit like the gated communities above with a time-share option, and they are commonly found in the beach communities with medium- to high-density tourism. The administration acts as your property manager and will market and maintain your home. You pay fees to cover common areas, security and upkeep but with luck, your rentals will cover these and more.

There are typically three kinds of time share available:

1. - **Fixed week**: having access to the same week every year. This is the most popular option and is the most expensive to buy into.

2. - **Floating week**: you sign up for a certain week without the guarantee that it will be available.

3. - **Random week**: a week is given to the timeshare holder without any choice, making it inconvenient for people on rigid work schedules.

Buying into this kind of resort might mean paying more for the unit, but if you only intend to use the place as a vacation spot for several weeks per year, it can be good deal. You can expect to make a purchase payment of between US$5K –10K that will give you one- to two-weeks' use of the unit.

On top of that you will pay maintenance fees that reach US$100 per month. Up in the Guanacaste hot spots of Flamingo and Tamarindo, some condos can rent out for US$1,000 a week in high season, which would more than cover your initial and running costs.

Even for private condos without all the sports or hotel amenities, renting out your unit has never been easier with the greater influx of tourists desperate for a beach-side vacation.

There is a current shortage of accommodation for visitors as demand has outstripped supply and the problem is becoming more acute. However, time share in Costa Rica is open to misinterpretation and some who have taken this route find they are landed with other heavy annual fees and constricting regulations. You must check out the conditions and regulations thoroughly and what your expenditures are going to be.

Costa Ricans are named *Ticos* because they tend to add the diminutive to many of the words they use. Instead of ordering a *chico* (small) dessert, they will ask for a *chiquitico* dessert or a *postrecito* instead of *postre*, which may make it sound less fattening (?) If you are learning Spanish and hear the ...*tico* at the end of something, focus on translating the first part of the word.

Buying or Building To Rent. If you decide to build for yourself, why not add on a couple of extra units to rent out? If you have the space on your plot of land, and the zoning regulations allow for additional residential units, this is an option that could give you some useful extra income.

Since you are already building your own home, you have the construction gangs and architect at hand and you should be able to negotiate some good deals on bulk-bought building materials as well as agreeing on a diminishing rate-per-unit charge for architect's plans and even legal fees.

Chapter Eight

Bed And Breakfast Business

It sounds like the perfect combination: live in a beautiful home that also earns you money. Offer some rooms out and add in breakfast and you're in business. **Well, it isn't quite like that.** One of the biggest misconceptions about the Bed & Breakfast business is that it is an easy option.

Many ex-pats without any experience or preparation at all try to set up a B&B and when it fails, they are confused and upset. Who do they blame? Costa Rica! That is just plain unfair. The highly successful B&Bs run by foreigners here testify to a satisfying and income-earning job. But it comes with hard work, dedication and market and personal research.

Ginette Laurin, who runs a popular recommended B&B, *Casa Laurin* started out with one suitcase, a thin wallet and a **big dream** in 2000 and five years later still admits to learning while enjoying her "Lifestyle" kind of inn keeping. Our thanks to Ginette of **costa-rica-bed-and-breakfast.com** for the following expert information on managing a B&B.

Why are there so many successful Mexicans, Colombians and other Latin Americans living in Costa Rica? Learn by reading our articles at **WeLoveCostaRica.com**.

Is Inn Keeping A Lifestyle, A Business Or A Hobby?

It is important to identify the type of inn keeping you want:

- Lifestyle

- Business

- Hobby, or a combination thereof.

Since we all had a "past life", be honest with yourself and review your natural and learned skills as well as areas where you may require assistance to keep up with an innkeeper's 24-hour-on-duty lifestyle.

If you plan to share the pleasures of inn keeping with a life or business partner, you may want to do the review that follows individually and compare results. Give yourself a score (1-10) on the topics listed below. Of course, anything you feel is just *not you* can be adjusted to your style or you can assign it to someone else, such as your spouse, business partner or hired help. To trigger the evaluation process, these questions might be useful.

- Who am I? – **What are my strengths** and weaknesses?

- **What do I like to do?** What do I find easy and moderately easy to do?

- What is it **I don't like to do** and requires discipline when I need to do it?

- What is it I don't want to do or **don't have the ability** to do?

- Am I **willing to learn Spanish?**

Good Health, High Energy

Can you take care of your physical, mental and spiritual Self (take time to *fill up your tank*) while offering TLC and full customer service to your guests? Are you a morning person – **can you smile when you get up** and enjoy your guests before your first cup of coffee? Can you go to bed late and wake up early four nights in a row? Can you take vacation time every year?

What about single women living in Costa Rica? What's it like for them? You can learn more by reading our articles at **WeLoveCostaRica.com**

Unconditional Love Of Mankind

Can you have someone in your space many hours every day? Can you adapt to other cultures? Are you interested in learning about other people's life experience? **Can you accept the differences?** Can you be around people who think they know it all or people who need to be guided? Are you open to learning from every circumstance in your life?

Organization

Can you handle multiple tasks? Can you prioritize, coordinate, delegate? Are you curious? Can you be creative? Can you make the best of everything? Can you look for solutions and stay positive? Can you keep things simple? **Are you patient** or do you need to learn to be patient? Are you good at bookkeeping? Marketing? Are you up to reading or filling out long information sheets in Spanish?

Love Your Staff

Can you learn from your helpers? Can you treat your staff as you would like to be treated? Can you say: I love you!? Can you appreciate your staff's commitment? **Are you willing to train your staff** to your standards…and train them again? Are you willing to accept that individual perceptions guide people's behavior? Can you be specific in your requests?

Value-For-Money Gourmet Food

Are you a chef? Can you adapt menus to guests' food restrictions or preferences? Do you cook with love…or just salt and pepper? Can you manage a fridge? Would you rather order in when you have visitors? Do you think that guests will come back for the quality or presentation of your dishes without impeccable service? Can you plan a feast at a price you can afford?

If your results show you are an unadulterated Business-oriented innkeeper, your business drive and skills have probably already taken care of the details. After a thorough survey, you must have on hand your business plan with a five-year action strategy by now.

If you have discovered that you are a genuine Hobby sort of innkeeper, make sure you move to Costa Rica with enough money to support yourself, invite your friends and family to put in a good word for you and enjoy the ride!

Ginette considers herself a Lifestyle B&B person, and you might be one too. She also firmly believes that learning Spanish is mandatory and part of the process to being a successful innkeeper in Costa Rica.

The location you choose (city vs. country, beach vs. mountain) will impact the type of guest, turnover, length of stay and other aspects of your business but remember that **the first person to enjoy or endure the environment is you**. Let your body guide you – it knows where it is going to be content and comfortable.

In Ginette's view the **Lifestyle option is a condition, not a goal.** Living in an environment where you are happy, you will attract the type of guests who are looking for the same atmosphere – see, you already have something in common when they arrive! The first contact is established!

Of course, there are still a zillion other issues involved in buying the Inn and establishing your contacts, marketing and operations, etc. If all this sounds exciting, there are other great sources of information, one of them being a

seminar offered by the Costa Rica Innkeepers' Association
(costaricainnkeepers.com)

Some properties may have restrictions. You may be able to buy 1,000 m2 (10,760 ft2) of land but you need to be sure how much construction is allowed on that land! If you're only allowed to build a 150-m2 (1,615-ft2) house, when you wanted to build a 300-m2 (3,228-ft2) home, you will be disappointed. You must get a *uso de suelo* report from the *Municipalidad* (Local Authority) which will inform you of any and all restrictions.

Chapter Nine

Building

Before you can build, you need somewhere to be able to build. The piece of land you choose in Costa Rica will fall into one of two categories. One normally involves a straightforward transaction (**titled land**): the other can create a bundle of trouble for you (**land without title**).

The Land: With Or Without Title

Land With Title. Everything you have read so far about the *Registro Nacional* and properties registered there deals with titled land. The majority of properties in urban areas, especially in the Central Valley will have title. Wherever possible, **this is the kind of property to buy** since the systems are in place to validate ownership and any conditions attached to it.

Land without Title. Usually undeveloped, old agricultural or rural plots of land or beach concessions, untitled land is best avoided if you don't want complications. **Untitled land cannot be registered** in the *Registro Nacional*, which is your main security proving ownership as well as providing details of its history, liens and encumbrances.

Land ownership without title cannot be legally verified except through a complicated judicial action called *información posesoria* (proof of possession).

This can relate to land that has been in a person's continuous and bona fide *possession* for ten years before presenting it for registration, or someone who takes over the rights of possession from a previous *possessor*.

The possessor must not know of anyone else with a better right of possession, which constitutes an act of trust and would seem impossible to prove. However, to validate the claim, **three neighbors must agree** in court supporting the possessor's claim and agreeing to the boundaries.

- Land designated for public use or with restrictions such as being in a forestry or nature reserve cannot be registered.

- The court inspects the property.

- A notice is placed in the official government news sheet, *La Gaceta,* publicly notifying a claim to the land.

- If no counter claims appear, the possessor wins his case and the court orders a writ (*mandamiento*) to the *Registro Nacional* to register the land.

- Once registered, the land might fall subject to further easements and restrictions as part of a general development plan (water rights, public-road development, etc.).

Only after the ten-year period can the land can be registered in the *Registro Nacional.*

You would have to want that piece of land really badly to take on those odds! Even once a piece of formally untitled land reaches the *Registro*, there is a three-year period when third parties can lay claim to the land and nothing is really sure until ten years after registration.

Beware of 'mediocre' neighborhoods! The area could improve but then again, the neighborhood could go into a major decline. You would be much better off buying property where your chances of success are higher.

How Do I Start?

First, take a deep breath! Buying a house is stressful enough - you are putting out all that money and you don't want to get ripped off. The worry can be even greater since all the documentation is in Spanish. But building your own place - that can feel like a huge step into the void!

The most important first step to take is to **analyze sincerely and honestly** whether this is the right route for you to take.

- If you want an American-style, luxury-fitted mansion, don't expect to pay much less than in the US. Some things are much cheaper here but if you have to import special brand-name bathroom and kitchen fittings, you must factor in the extra costs of getting them here.

- If you don't speak Spanish, who is going to help you communicate with the architect, real estate lawyer, site foreman and suppliers?

- If you have never had experience building in your home country where there may be tighter building codes and more understandable procedures, are you patient and persistent enough to make a go of it in Costa Rica?

Let's assume you have spotted your plot of land. It is just what you want. The right size, great location and the price is good. So what do you have to do next?

When evaluating places to live, remember that most *Ticos* have a **much higher tolerance for noise** than you probably have. Check the area for barking dogs and strange sounds at different times at night as well as during the day. You may not want to visit at 3 am but it's preferable to buying a home and finding out on your first night that your neighbor has a sawmill in his back garden that he only uses when he gets home after finishing his day job.

Getting A Building Permit

There are several things you need to research on your piece of land before applying for a building permit:

- **What basic services** does the plot have? Access to water, electricity, telephone, drains?

- **What restrictions** and conditions apply to the land? This could be future roads, zoning plans or environmental conditions, especially if your land is near a natural or forestry reserve or was formally agricultural land.

With this information, you apply for a building permit at the Permit Office (*Oficina Receptora de Permisos de Construcción*). Your application will be checked by the multiple government departments controlling building permits:

- The Ministry of Public Work (*Ministerio de Obras Pública* MOPT);

- National Institute for Housing and Urbanization (*Instituto Nacional de Vivienda y Urbanismo* INVU);

- Costa Rica Institute for Energy (*Instituto Costarricense de Energía* ICE);

- Costa Rica Water Authority (*Instituto Costarricense de Acueductos y Alcantarillados* AYA);

151

- National Electricity Service (*Servicio Nacional de Electricidad* SNE);

- Federated Association of Engineers and Architects (*Colegio Federado de Ingenieros y Arquitectos* CFIA);

- Ministry of Health (*Ministerio de Salud*).

All of them have to approve your plans. It pays to get them right first time.

If you plan on building a **house bigger than 70 m2 (753 ft2)** (and surely most of you will), you must present the following:

- 4 copies - building plans;

- 4 copies - survey plan (*plano catastrado*);

- 4 copies - permit checklist (*hoja de comisión*);

- 2 copies – deeds;

- 1 copy - consulting contract with architect or engineer (*contrato de consultoría*);

- Approval from the water authority, AYA, about water availability;

- 1 copy - electrical plan approved by SNE.

With all that in hand you can then apply for a building permit from the local municipal authority where your land is located. They are legally responsible for making sure your construction complies with the building regulations for that municipality. You can expect to be inspected by a local municipal inspector during your construction.

> What's the **dating scene like for singles** in Costa Rica? You can learn more by reading our articles at **WeLoveCostaRica.com**

Who Can Help You Get All This Paperwork Together?

Your lawyer can help but unless he specializes in conveyance, he may lack the contacts to smooth over the whole process. An architect, on the other hand, is working with this stuff every day. He will know his way around municipal offices and departments. However, don't expect him to do this automatically; **this must be established at the outset** and factored into his fee scale.

Finding An Architect Or Civil Engineer

Now you need to find an architect or civil engineer to create your dream home. Almost as important as your doctor, **he or she will be your lifeline** and will look after you and your interests. You need to establish a close, trusting relationship, with open, honest communication.

If you can't tell your architect what you want in design details, how is he expected to find out - telepathy? This is a delicate relationship because if you are dealing with a *Tico* architect or engineer, **there will be innate cultural differences** influencing styles, layouts, room sizes on both sides.

What about the theatre? Movies? What is there to do while living in Costa Rica? Learn more by reading our articles at
WeLoveCostaRica.com

Existing building standards in the US pre-determine the whole building process. In Costa Rica, you will find that things are much more lenient and you might find yourself overwhelmed by the style options available to you. If that is the case, then listen to your architect and trust in his judgment on the structural demands of your house.

All **architects and engineers must be licensed** (unlike brokers!) and are affiliated to the Costa Rican Federated College of Engineers and Architects (*Colegio Federado de Ingenieros y Arquitectos* or CFIA). Ask to see their license from the Association as some unlicensed, mostly foreign, architects are operating in the country and you will have no recourse should you run into problems with them.

Affiliation to the Association (or Colegio) means the architect has to be responsible for his actions. If a claim is filed against him, the Colegio acts as moderator and judge and if found liable, an architect could lose his license for up to two years and you as client are entitled to compensation.

As with any relationship, you may not hit it off first time. This is a long-term involvement and both sides want to come through it still on speaking terms. Don't despair! Brian Timmons, who is building a residential complex in Santa Ana (**residenciaslosjardines.com**) met with nearly 20 architects before finding the professional that suited him, his needs and his budget.

From among those 20, he received quotes for plans ranging from US$1,500 to US$66,000 – for the same housing units!

What is the difference between an architect and a civil engineer? According to Elias Robles, an English-speaking architect working in the Central Valley

153

and Guanacaste and collaborating with Brian, the engineer will create a wonderfully solid structure but it may look like a jailhouse; an architect has more of an eye for the aesthetics. Unless you can convey your design concepts clearly to an engineer, it will probably be easier to work with an architect.

The Association establishes fees these professionals can charge for different stages of construction and the services they provide, and they are similar for both architects and engineers. The fees are negotiable, but have been established as a yardstick to protect both professionals and clients.

There are **no *required* inoculations** for Costa Rica, but consult with your doctor for recommendations of optional inoculations and health precautions. Some areas of Costa Rica are more tropical than others and you may need more protection if you are planning on visiting those areas.

There have been cases of clients trying to cut costs by hiring a draftsman to draw up cheaper plans, having them 'officially signed' for presentation by an architect to the *Colegio* and avoiding paying the full fees for professionally drawn-up plans.

As with your dealings with a broker and real estate attorney, you must be clear what the architect is going to do for you. If a language problem exists, **get an agreement down in writing** and have it translated, so there are no doubts as to the services offered. Even if you do speak Spanish, this is a wise step to take.

Elias Robles comments that some foreigners are only too quick to blame the architect when the house doesn't turn out as planned – according to the client. Without technical know-how, or good communications skills or the language to convey ideas, it is unfair to blame the architect if he proceeds with whatever little information he has.

Some Factors To Consider:

- Communication.

- **Try to get it right first time.** Making changes are costly.

- Unless you are a fluent Spanish speaker, find a bilingual architect and have the agreement drawn up in both languages.

- Request computer-image plans of your house so you can 'walk through' a 3-D image.

- Be prepared to buy local fittings and use local materials for better servicing and replacement.

All foreigners visiting or living in Costa Rica should be prepared to present to Costa Rican authorities proof of their legal entry and stay in Costa Rica. This proof can be a photocopy of the appropriately stamped tourist card or passport. If you are planning on staying over the maximum (usually 90 days), this extended stay must be authorized by immigration authorities.

Building Plans And Permits

Two main phases make up a construction project and fees are a percentage based on the value of the project: building Plans and permits with four sections, and construction and supervision with three sections.

1. Preliminary Study- 0.5% of project cost. This isn't obligatory and it depends on how complex your construction designs are going to be.

2. Pre-construction Draft Design - 1% to 1.5%. Spend time with this stage. Your architect or engineer will sit down with you and discuss what you want and need. This stage is vital because he will prepare the draft plans your construction assuming you agree with them.

It will be **frustrating and costly to make changes** afterwards so you need all your communication skills to express just what you want from your construction. Once plans are drawn up, they will include the site plan and preliminary drawings for your review and approval. Not many of us are expert at visualizing what paper plans will look like in reality. Ask your architect to give you a 3-D virtual overview on a computer, so you can *walk through* your house and *see* what the windows and doors will look like and whether the bedroom is big enough for two children.

3. Final Construction Plans and Technical Specifications - 4% of project cost. Based on the draft plans, the architect now draws up the final Plans upon which your house will be constructed. It is important you are satisfied with them! Later on is not the time to change. The completed set of plans must be approved by the Costa Rican Association of Engineers and Architects and need to include:

- Site plan
- Distribution plan
- Elevation, transversal and longitude perspectives
- Roof design with guttering

- Design of footings and support beams
- Structural plans
- Electrical layout
- Mechanical and sanitary layout
- Interior fittings and finishings.

4. Budget - 0.5% for a global budget; 1% for itemized costs. Your architect then gives you a list of materials based on your discussions and will prepare a construction budget.

Are there any deadly diseases and dangerous insects in Costa Rica you need to worry about? You can learn more by reading our articles at **WeLoveCostaRica.com**

Construction And Supervision

Three options are open to you as to what kind of supervision you would like, depending on how much involvement you want the architect or engineer to have during construction.

- **Inspection** (*Inspección*). Your architect or engineer visits at least once a week to make sure the general contractor is following the plans. He also checks that the correct materials are being used and goes over the invoices. (3% of total construction cost.)

- **Technical Supervision** (*Dirección Supervisión*). The architect visits daily and is more directly involved with the step-by-step details of construction. (5% of total construction cost.)

- **Administration** (*Administración*). The architect manages the whole project and takes total responsibility for its completion. (12% total construction costs.)

You are talking about large amounts of money here. Your costs for both these phases can be up to 16% if you go for the full range of services.

If you have the time, language and interest, you can involve yourself more closely with the construction and only require minimum supervision from your architect or engineer. And since this is Costa Rica and nobody is averse to some gentle bargaining, you could negotiate expenses with your architect for a *package* of fees that can reduce the individual costs substantially.

Whatever you set up, however, you must have the **contract looked over by your attorney**. Make sure you fully understand how much you are going to be paying out and how and when you are expected to pay and exactly what services you are going to receive.

Need to find out how much you should expect to pay your maid? Other employees? You can learn more by reading our articles at **WeLoveCostaRica.com**

The Building Contractors

The architect you choose can help you find an experienced, reliable contractor for your construction and naturally, it is to your benefit if they know each other and work well together. Many architects and engineers, even though they work independently, may also manage contracting companies that can provide the labor. However, **don't be trapped by a single option.** This stage involves a three-way relationship between you as client, the architect and the construction foreman (*Maestro de Obras*).

Whichever way you choose, here are some basic tips to help avoid building-site blues:

The **key person on site is the foreman.** He is the go-between for you as owner and the workforce that will put up your house. Get his credentials and references if possible from previous clients. Some foremen may have diplomas from the National Institute (*Instituto Nacional de Aprendizaje*), which look fine on paper but are no real guarantee of competence and no replacement for experience. If he's a drunk and a loudmouth, you need to know beforehand and make your decision accordingly.

The foreman controls his workforce and they can be a rough bunch at times. Many *Nicas* (illegal Nicaraguan laborers) are brought in for cheap labor and their habits might annoy neighbors living near to your building site. If there are blaring radios, loud expletive-filled conversations and catcalls being yelled from the rooftops at your neighbors' daughters, you will get complaints. The foreman is also in charge of the supplies coming onto the site and arranging delivery of materials. You need to decide whether it is best for him to have a credit line at the building merchants or are you prepared to go back and forth every time another fifty bags of cement are needed?

Learn to **be a good negotiator.** You are the owner, but you need to have a respectful, working relationship with your foreman. Discuss any problems of site conduct with him but also play fair with him. Make sure you, or your architect, pay on time for wages and materials and see that they have the basics, like a latrine and somewhere to wash and rest for lunch under shelter.

Would you like to see a few examples of different types of homes for sale in Costa Rica? You can see more at **WeLoveCostaRica.com**

Keep a **close watch on your materials** in case someone decides to 'remove' them. This is no worse in Costa Rica than in the US or Europe and is one of those 'hidden' costs factored into any construction plan. But there is no need to be gullible. It makes sense to ensure that the foreman has some kind of control system in place to log tools in and out, and don't deliver your expensive door knobs and faucets until they will be actually fitted.

Visit the site regularly; check on quality. Don't interfere with the workers and any complaints you have, do it through your foreman. If you have opted for the Technical Supervision or Administration package with your architect, then you address any concerns through him.

Theoretically, construction should be regularly inspected by the municipal building authorities but the reality can be otherwise. This largely depends on the zone you choose, and some inspectors are more than laid-back about rigorously checking construction in their patch. You might well not have more than a couple of inspections during the course of your whole building process. However, it goes without saying that you should still adhere to the requisite building norms for your zone.

Escazú in particular has become the wealthiest municipal authority largely because of the building frenzy it has allowed. The result is chaos! Public services and the roads can't cope with the uncontrolled condos and residential estates being put up, but the income generated is too good to miss and the rules and zoning restrictions aren't always strictly applied.

Alternative Construction Options

Construction options and house styles are as varied as the plot of land you choose and Costa Rica is no exception. Just around San José, two 'alternative' building systems offer a different construction approach from the more usual block-and-beam style. Although they might not come in that much cheaper per square meter when comparing material costs, both offer **much faster construction timeframes**, which in themselves translate into substantial savings.

Would you like the *Inside Scoop* on people who have already moved to Costa Rica and are enjoying their lives? You can learn more by reading our articles at **WeLoveCostaRica.com**

Log-Built Homes

One company between San José and Cartago offers a complete construction package for their clients who yearn for a log-built chalet.

The company's team of in-house experts help obtain necessary building permits, carry out topographical surveys and soil studies, prepare computerized architectural plans and oversee the final finish on homes. Their catalog is ample proof of the great variety of styles possible, with the client's pocketbook and imagination the only limitations.

Building with wood is not a new idea if you come from Canada or the States, but **log homes have found a niche** in Costa Rica. Purpose-grown eucalyptus and pine are cut at four years once a 15-cm diameter is reached. At the processing facility, the trunks are debarked and smoothed then dried in special cylindrical kilns in a vacuum and preserving agents are added at a pressure of 12 kg/cm2 to ensure maximum penetration.

The dried, treated trunks repel insects, fungal growth and sun damage with the chemicals also acting as fire retardant to withstand 420°C (788°F), which is kind of useful when you have chosen an open fireplace!

The chemical agents comply with international norms (The American Wood Preservers' Association) and are non-toxic. Arsenic is not applied in any areas to be used by humans and the company claims the wood as **good for up to fifty years.**

Per square meter of construction, the costs are below traditional standard housing prices, which vary between US$400 - 700 m2 ($37 – 65 ft2). The log-built homes are about US$270 - 310 m2 ($25 – 29 ft2) including services installation, bathroom fittings, tiled flooring, kitchen fittings and hot water.

Pre-Fabricated Modular Systems

Pre-fabricated vertical concrete panels of various dimensions reinforced with steel bars provide a **fast way of house assembly** that can cut construction time by over half when compared to traditional cement block-built systems.

Panel widths vary between 25 to 50 cm with a uniform height of 2.75 m (9 feet) and 6.35 cm thickness. Internal wall height is 2.45 m (8 feet). Since the steel reinforced corner columns are the same 6.35 cm thickness, they do not jut out from the wall as often happens in other pre-fab houses giving smooth uniform interior wall surfaces. Interior walls can be made either of the concrete panels or a cheaper option is lightweight gypsum.

The foundation is made of a 25-cm-thick concrete frame reinforced with rebar at 250 kg/cm2 resistance. Steel rebar angles embedded in the foundations literally hook the wall panels to the platform, which insures an integral strength in the whole construction. The main joists joining walls to roof can be made of wood, perling or cement. The hollows created by the half-moon channel ends of each panel are filled with a fine mortar mix or expanding concrete to fuse them and insure impermeability. Panel joins are unnoticeable once covered with a smooth cement-acrylic plaster that comes either pre-stained in a choice of colors or plain to be later painted or papered.

A fairly straightforward single-storey two-bedroom house takes about 60 days to complete from the time the contract is signed to moving in, as opposed to five to seven months with block and beam. Cost per meter for a completed house with all wiring and plumbing, basic kitchen and bathroom fittings and tiled flooring is around US$330 m2 ($30 ft2).

Are you supposed to be paying taxes while living in Costa Rica? You can learn more by reading our articles at **WeLoveCostaRica.com**

Water In Your Well And In Your House

If you have decided on a piece of paradise outside main municipal services, the most fundamental service you are going to need is water. Without access to reliable, clean water for you, your house and garden, paradise could turn into hell.

Obviously we recommend that your chosen architect, if you decide to build in the *boonies,* knows about finding water on your land and drilling wells, or at least can find the right person for the job. It is a highly specialized area of expertise.

We thank Jerry and Ana Werth, who own and run a water well contracting company, *Pura Vida,* for the following expert advice on not just finding water but the local laws pertaining to groundwater access.

Your land may already have a well on it. If so, then ideally you should check it before completing the final transaction to ensure it can still provide enough sweet water for your needs. If this is not so, you need to improve on the existing well, or dig a new one.

Salinity Study. If the property is within one kilometer (0.62 mile) of the high tide mark you will need a *Intrusion de Salina* study performed by an independent registered geologist to ensure your water well will not perforate the salt water table and allow co-mingling of the two aquifers. He will visit your site and make recommendations on the depth and well construction. He then makes out a complete report that is attached and submitted to the local authorities with your permit application.

Digging the Well. Jerry charges $100.00 per meter drilled. This price includes everything to complete a standard water well excluding the submersible pumping system. All wells are constructed according to American standards. Installation can be with 5–12″-diameter PVC casing to a maximum of 300 m using rotary or percussion drilling units. The cost includes well casing, screen, top and end caps and sanitary seal.

Permits. Documents needed for a permit are proof you are the owner of the property, a copy of your *plano catastro*, your identification papers and if property is owned by a corporation, the *cédula jurídica* assigned to this corporation. It usually takes about 60 days to get approval for a water well and costs US$250 through Pura Vida.

Final Report. **Once your well is dug, a final report is prepared** giving the specific details of your well with geologic conditions, water levels, well capacity, well specifications and general site observations. This report has a charge of $150.00 and is due at the completion of your well.

Cost of a well:	US$
• geologist's report, *intrusion de salina*	300
• well perforation x meter	100
• permit	300
• mobilization	500
• per diem x two crew/day	50
• pump test x two hours 150 psi/400 cfm	250
• access if necessary x hour	100
• final report	150

Depth Guarantee. Although the company can guarantee depth, it cannot guarantee the presence of water. In the case of a dry hole being drilled, a charge is made of 50% of the cost proposed.

Pura Vida Drilling and Well Service is a full-service water-well contracting company owned by Jerry and Ana Werth. Jerry has over 18 years of drilling experience with a degree in environmental science specializing in soil and groundwater contamination. Ana is an expert in water-well permits and Costa Rican laws pertaining to groundwater laws.

If you would like to contact Jerry and Ana for more information on well drilling, log onto **WeLoveCostaRica.com** and click on Contact U

Chapter Ten

Life On The Beach

Many retirees coming into Costa Rica dream about a beachfront house, looking out over the ocean all ready for a peaceful and leisurely retirement. There is nothing wrong with this wish - in theory. In practice, though, buying beachfront land or a house falls into a category all its own and **special restrictions apply** (just about the only ones) for foreigners. We touched on untitled land in Chapter Nine, **Building**, but the law and legal restrictions surrounding beachfront properties merit careful study.

The Shoreline Zone Law (*Ley sobre la Zona Marítimo Terrestre*)

The *Zona Marítimo* covers 200 meters (656 feet): the first 50 meters (164 feet) measured from the high tide mark are public (*zona pública*) and **no private development can take place** except officially approved marinas and port facilities.

The next 150 meters 492 feet) inland are called the concessionary zone (*zona restringida*) and land falling in this zone can be leased only, never bought freehold, for private development. Most property of this kind is untitled; the Costa Rica government owns this zone and it is managed by the local municipalities who oversee the concessionary zone and issue special leases for private use.

Do not think of these leases as standard leaseholds; they are more like a right of use (concession) for a fairly short time. You can build here with conditions, but once your lease falls due and it isn't renewed, any infrastructure reverts to the municipal authority.

Owning property near the beach can be complicated and certain restrictions apply to foreigners buying property near the beach. According to the Shoreline Zone Law the first 50 meters (164 feet) above the tide's highest point cannot be used for anything but public use and nothing can be built in this area either. The 150 meters (492 feet) after that can be leased (five to twenty years) for private use but this will revert back to the municipality after the termination of the lease. So if someone tries to tell you they have some incredible property right 'on the beach' for sale – be warned!

Leases usually run for between five to twenty years and you can apply for renewal. Once the lease or concession has been granted, it is registered in the special registry section of the *Registro Nacional* called *Registro de Concesiones de la Zona Marítimo Terrestre*. Once you have the concession, **you must pay an annual fee for the concession**.

As a foreigner, you must have had legal residency status in Costa Rica for at least five years before applying and being granted a concession in this zone. If you have less than five years' residency, you cannot have more than a 50% interest in a beachfront property. If you wish to lease land through a company, it cannot have more than 50% foreign ownership.

Concessions cannot be granted to:

- foreigners who have not lived in Costa Rica for at least five years;
- corporations with shareholders;
- foreign-registered companies;
- companies wholly made up of foreigners;
- companies with invested capital or shares provided by more than 50% foreigners.

The maritime zone limits must be marked out by the National Geographic Institute (*Instituto Nacional Geográfico*) and a development plan must also be drafted and approved with government and municipal endorsement. Without official approval, you might find yourself leasing land that has no development permit.

If there is no **zoning plan, you are responsible** for making one and submitting it to the Costa Rica Tourist Board (*Instituto Costarricense de Turismo* ICT), and Housing and Urban Development Department (*Instituto Nacional de Vivienda e Urbanización* INVU) and the relevant local municipal authority for approval. Is it worth it? That's for you to decide!

The Golfo de Papagayo with its huge Papagayo Peninsula Project is covered by a special tourism development plan and it comes under different regulations as can shorefront that falls within some beach town limits.

Why do *Ticas* (Costa Rican women) like Americans? You can learn more by reading our articles at **WeLoveCostaRica.com**

The King Of Spain's Lands

It sounds like something out of the storybooks, but some *very few* shorefront properties were given special title by the King of Spain way back in colonial times. These lands have purchasing title granted down to the water and out into the ocean as far as a horse can wade up to its belly. It's a quaint old story and if anyone tries to sell you land and strings this line, then be warned, the offer is *nearly always* going to be a fairytale too!

Is The Beach The Right Place For You?

After visiting one of Costa Rica's many **beautiful beaches** on vacation, many people rush to the conclusion, "Wouldn't it be nice to live here?" However, beach living isn't for everyone and enjoying a one-week vacation with a piña colada in hand watching the sunset is not the same as living at the beach.

Costa Rica is still a developing country and although you will find all of the modern conveniences in San José and the surrounding Central Valley towns, the beach areas do not have that kind of infrastructure.

Apart from the extra complications explained above of buying beachfront property, here are some other considerations to bear in mind, put together by people who know what living on the beach is like:

- All **serious business** is done in San José.

- Beaches are 90 minutes - 5 hours from San José.

- There are **no good hospitals near the beach** - none!

- Real estate prices in *hot* beach areas are the highest in the country.

- The *hottest* real estate areas tend to have more crime.

- Buying properly titled land can be complicated.

- Getting building permits can be more complicated.

- The beach environment is **tough on your home**.

- **Everything rusts** - corrosion affects your car and home appliances.

- Beach areas can be hot, humid and **air conditioning costs add up**.

- There are **more insects** at the beach.

- Getting a telephone line installed can take a very long time.

- Cellular telephone coverage is limited.

- Fast internet access is not available in 99% of beach areas.

- Some beaches have unhealthy levels of pollution.

- Dining out, groceries and utilities are **more expensive** than San José.

- There is literally only one good fully international school (and it's expensive) in Guanacaste.

- Cultural activities, entertainment and nightlife are limited.

- Good dentists and other professionals can be **hard to find**.

- Warranty work required for your car **must be done in San José**.

- The **roads can be a 'challenge'** and this will also affect your car.

- Fresh food is harder to find and does not stay fresh for long.

- Overall, your **cost of living will be higher** than San José.

What different religions can be found in Costa Rica? You can learn more by reading our articles at **WeLoveCostaRica.com**

Now, some people living on the beach do *not want* modern facilities and urban development and if you also have that *pioneer* attitude, Costa Rica **beach living may be perfect for you**.

For most of us accustomed to such conveniences, however, the lack of facilities can be a marvelous escape from 'civilization' during a short vacation but, after six months of driving four hours every week just to stock up on our favorite groceries, life in the back of beyond can get tiring.

What do most people do? When we want to go to the beach, we hop into our cars, drive for a few hours and we're there! For us, staying at a new, exotic and different beach location each time is worry-free and beats the pants off spending all that money on a home in the same place that we won't use nearly as much as we think we will. And how often will you actually go to the beach anyway?

So it's one thing to visit the beach; actually living there is a whole different ball game. So, please, if you are seriously thinking about beach living and have any doubts whatsoever, **may we suggest** that you live there for six months and **rent first**.

If you are absolutely convinced beach living is right for you after that time then take a look around the area you now know really well and find a suitable property to buy!

Chapter Eleven

Looking After Your Real Estate

Home Insurance

Our thanks to David Garrett of Garrett & Associates for his expert home insurance information that follows. Should you wish to communicate with David, please visit his website at **segurosgarrett.com**

So now you have your Costa Rica home. You have closed the deal, locked all the papers safely away and paid off the bills. You might think it is time to sit back and relax but don't head for your hammock just yet.

Although Costa Rica is much more secure than other nations in the region, burglary can happen, natural disasters do occur and if you go away for the weekend with the toaster oven still on, you could return to a pile of ashes.

The national insurance company, INS (*Instituto Nacional de Seguros*) happens to be a monopoly so there's no point in shopping around. However, finding a good insurance broker can help smooth things over should you ever have to make a claim. If you want to insure your house and/or its contents, there are several ways you can do this. You can also have a Liability policy, in case someone sues you for an accident occurring in your abode.

The long-standing company of Garrett & Associates has years of experience helping English-speaking residents with their insurance needs and has itemized this information for insuring your property.

It is recommended that you register at your Embassy when you do settle down in Costa Rica. Not only is this good for your peace of mind in the event of an emergency but your government also gets to know where to find you when they want to raise your taxes.

Home Fire & Natural Disaster Policy (*Hogar Seguro 2000*).

This is for homes and/or their contents. It can only be used for single dwellings, not commercial buildings or apartments. If the house is rented, the tenant covers his household effects and the landlord insures the house itself.

Within this policy, there are four "sub-coverages":

- **A** covers fire and lightning;
- **B** covers damage caused by mutiny, strikes, vandalism, hurricane, cyclone, explosion, smoke, falling objects, vehicles and resulting fire;
- **C** pays for damage caused by floods and landslides;
- **D** covers natural disasters: earthquakes, tremors, volcanoes, tsunamis, etc.

C and **D** are sold jointly. You can take **A** coverage by itself, **A+B**, **A+CD**, or complete coverage **A+B+CD**.

Premium is based on the value of what is being insured, and it is up to you, the applicant, to come up with reasonable values. The house can be based on Depreciated New Value, i.e. estimated cost of rebuilding, less 1% depreciation for every year of construction. The contents are based on Actual Cash Value (depreciated value) – what you would get at a garage sale. The insurance company, INS, does not ask for a comprehensive list, but you should itemize single articles worth US$750 or more.

Coverage **A** costs 0.0672% of the value. **A+B** costs 0.0896%. **A+CD** costs 0.2212%. Complete coverage **A+B+CD** costs 0.2436%. In addition, premiums are taxed 13%. Example of all-in cost: **A+B+CD** for a US$100,000 home would cost US$243.60 per year, plus 13% tax equals US$275.27. Most people buy **ABCD**.

Deductibles. On **B** coverage the deductible is 20,000 colones per claim. For hurricane damage it is 20% with a minimum of 20,000 colones. For **C** and **D** coverages the deductible is 1% of the total insured amount with a minimum of 50,000 colones. As is usual with INS policies, these deductibles are fixed and standard: no variations are possible.

INS has sold the *Hogar Seguro 2000* policy since 1988. It is a good policy for major disasters (don't claim for cigarette burns on your living room carpet!) and in the aftermath of the bad earthquakes of 1990 and 1991 INS responded fairly and efficiently in paying claims.

A recommendation: if you live in a non-combustible house (like most houses nowadays) don't insure the contents, which would hardly be affected in an earthquake –probably your major concern. If you live in a wood cabin or other potentially inflammable house - yes, you should insure the contents.

The numbering system for houses on streets can be confusing. On one street, we had houses with the following number sequence: 1, 3, 289, 291 then 99. So when you are looking for a specific house remember that #99 doesn't necessarily show up after #97.

Home Theft Insurance

This covers items stolen from within the house, in verifiable situations of breaking and entering – providing items appear on a list. You must list everything within the house - not just high-risk items like TVs and stereos. But you cannot insure jewelry, gems, precious metals, furs, cosmetics, cash, portable electronics, cameras, firearms, motor vehicles, animals, documents or securities.

INS specifies that they will only provide Theft insurance if the house is of "solid" construction, with double or deadbolt locks on outside doors, and with bars on the windows.

Your list should include Actual Cash Values in colones for all items, approximate dates of acquisition, and full descriptions of electrical items, cameras, mowers, bikes: makes, models, and serial numbers.

To Make a Claim. You must advise INS immediately by calling on (800) 800-3030. You will only be attended to in Spanish, so have a Spanish-speaking friend with you to help. A police report with a list of stolen items is mandatory, with copy for INS.

Paperwork is considerable and settlements usually take 60 days or more. The deductible is 10% of the value of stolen items with a minimum 50,000 colones per break in.

Damage to the home caused by thieves breaking and entering is paid up to 5% of the total insured value, and based on repair bills.

The premium rate depends on the security and location of the home: there are discounts for good security, and surcharges for remote locations. The average annual rate is 1.4% for the total years on the list, including 13% sales tax.

How does living in Costa Rica compare to Nicaragua or Guatemala? You can learn more by reading our articles at **WeLoveCostaRica.com**

Recommendations. It usually takes two to three weeks to get Theft insurance in place, so don't apply on the eve of your departure on a world cruise. This policy is extremely hard to claim against – there are lots of conditions, the most notorious of which translates as "If the building is to be unoccupied or its usual dwellers absent for a period of more than 48 hours, the insured must place it in the care of a guard. For periods greater than one month, in addition to hiring a guard, the Insured must inform INS in writing at least one week before the absence is to commence...." Installing a home alarm system sometimes makes sense!

What are the **Top Ten Gringo Legal Mistakes?** And are you about to make any of them? Learn more by reading our articles at **WeLoveCostaRica.com**

Homeowners' Liability Insurance

INS's *Responsabilidad Civil General* policy pays awards granted by the Court stemming from lawsuits due to accidents occurring in an insured premises or during an insured activity. This policy also covers legal costs if the Court rules that they should be paid by the insured.

Anyone can get this kind of insurance: homeowners, tour operators, hotels, restaurants, shops, food manufacturers. This policy is based on a certain activity or premises, and if foreseen that an accident may occur to a guest, consumer or client, a Liability policy may be advisable. Two coverages are available:

- Coverage **A** - Injury, loss of life and limb.
- Coverage **B** - Damage or loss of property.

You can have separate limits for coverage **A** and Coverage **B**, but the usual is a Combined Limit, where INS will pay up to the insured limit, per accident, regardless of the breakdown of the award. Try to visualize a worst-case scenario of what could happen in an accident: that is the recommended limit. Take into account, however, that in Costa Rica awards have not got out of hand, as in other countries, with regard to punitive damages, pain and suffering, and an assumption of deep pockets.

The premium is a percentage of the insured amount. For homeowners, it is usually around 1% per year. The exact rate is fixed by INS on a case basis, per the perceived risk as described on the policy application, which has to be filled out by the Agent when visiting the premises. It is usual, also, for INS to send an inspector, before establishing the rate, to look over the premises and verify information on the application.

Generally, Costa Rican judges have a **healthy attitude toward liability**, assuming that every person should exercise reasonable care to avoid accidents. This, coupled with the disregard of punitive damages, discourages Liability claims stemming from trivial accidents. Therefore, not many homeowners buy Liability policies. If a home is to be rented out, however, a small Liability policy may be in order.

Is it true what they say about the roads and driving in Costa Rica? You can learn more by reading our articles at
WeLoveCostaRica.com

Homeowners' Policy (*Hogar Seguro Comprensivo*)

INS started selling this policy in 2000. It comprises the Home Fire and the Home Theft policies. Without delving deeply, there are several things wrong with the Homeowners' policy:

- Only type "**A**" buildings can be insured. (Solid walls, in and out.) Houses with wooden or combustible walls – in and/or outside – are not eligible. All windows must be barred.

- All direct damage coverages (**ABCD** on the Home Fire policy) are automatically included. You cannot exclude any to save a few bucks.

- The contents must be insured for Theft, a coverage which most people eschew as it's very hard getting claims paid.

- The **contents must be insured** against natural disasters. People rarely insure contents, as earthquakes (most people's main fear) rarely damage them.

- **You must make – and keep updated** – a list of contents.

If none of the above disadvantages apply, a Homeowners' policy will save you some premium money. The standard rate is 0.893% applied to the total insured value – which is the sum of the Replacement Value for the house, and Actual Cash Value for the contents.

Costa Ricans may be delightful people but, they are **not the most careful drivers**. Many drivers consider red lights as 'optional' and will go straight through red lif they think there's no traffic. Having said that, traffic-accident rates have fallen for the fourth year running.

Looking After Your Home When You Are Not In Costa Rica

Once the excitement of owning Costa Rica property has settled down, it's time to get serious and think carefully about how you are going to make sure your Costa Rica real estate will be a safe and profitable investment.

If you don't intend on living full time in Costa Rica, you can contract experienced property management professionals to deal with your taxes, maintenance fees and bills, sort out rental contracts and many other services structured around your requirements. They can help ensure that your real estate is always in 'top-dollar' condition.

Why Do You Want Help With This?

When you buy property in a foreign country, there are many things you need to be aware of. You've already read that even the system of law in Costa Rica is completely different to what most people in North America are accustomed to and that could be a potentially dangerous difference if you don't know what you're doing and leave certain bills unpaid.

Taking care of even one property could be a full-time job for you if you don't know what you're up against. If you would prefer to have an expert taking care of all those headaches for you then read on.

Property Management Services

Just as you pay for any professional service, you need to pay for professional property management services too. However, a good company should give you the power and freedom to choose what services best fit your needs, taking care of all the important things (and some of the little things too) to maintain your property and its value to the highest standards.

If, say, you don't pay your municipal and annual property taxes on time, your house could be seized (*embargada*) by the state.

Also, if you live in a condominium and you don't pay the maintenance fee, the administrator can put you in *cobro judicial* which means that you will not be able to sell your home, no matter how attractive an offer you get, until that debt is paid and the Costa Rican government releases the house of any legal obligations.

Some property management companies work with all types of property, from single-family homes to multi-unit luxury condos and small commercial office spaces. A few provide a full range of remodeling and construction management services and, maximizing on their experience and connections, they will ensure that quality control and cost efficiency is a priority when making these improvements.

What you can expect to pay. Monthly fees can vary from around US$75 – 150, depending on the services chosen and the size of the property to be managed. A two-bedroom, two-bathroom house could cost you about $75 per month for basic housekeeping, inspection and payment of utility bills; pool maintenance is between $75 – 100 per year;

The different levels of service required depends on the kind of client, who fall into these main groups:

- Part-time resident, condo owner;

- Permanent resident, owner of individual unit;

- Part-time resident and occupier, not renting unit;

- Part-time occupiers, also renting out to vacationers;

- Investors renting out full-time.

Regular expenses must be covered, but some companies include an incidental expenses account in the budget since every building, at some point, requires redecoration or perhaps a major repair not included in your monthly maintenance fee.

Some of the services provided include:

- Paying bills

- Housekeeping

- Rent collection

- Security/inspection

- Structural Maintenance

- Landscape or garden maintenance

- Pool maintenance

- Car Maintenance

- Welcome Service.

Who will take care of paying utilities, taxes, insurance and any legal fees? You could face a lawsuit in Costa Rica if you forget to pay your property taxes, house and/or car insurance. And if you don't pay your service bills, you will be cut off. These can all be paid out of rents collected if you have chosen to rent your property.

Condo Owners. Condominium residents pay a maintenance fee. This charge varies, depending on what facilities you have. However, a typical service charge covers your security services, management and maintenance including gardening and preventive maintenance, cleaning of common areas and maintenance of the swimming pool. They inspect all work to ensure it is complete and up to their high standards.

Housekeeping. Whether you are living here or not, Costa Rica can get hot at times and your home must be cleaned regularly to avoid humidity problems that could damage furniture. You know how you feel when you walk into a sparkling, freshly cleaned home? Your home can be cleaned from top to bottom the day before you arrive, or on a weekly basis, whether the property is occupied or not..

Collecting Your Rent. Collecting the rent owed to you can sometimes be a 'challenge' and you must know what you can and cannot do. Global Concepts enforces all rules and regulations and takes care of service and all notices, as well as collections. They collect monthly rents from tenants on your behalf.

Who will take care of security? Do you really want to arrive at your home in Costa Rica tired after a long trip and discover that someone has broken into your house, stolen your car and your entertainment centre? A regular walk-through ensures everything is as it should be, and additional security measures can be taken as required.

Maintenance and Repairs. Property protection starts with a comprehensive visual and written record of the exact condition of the property. Periodic inspections ensure your property is being properly cared for, if rented, and with digital photography, these records can be maintained for accurate documentation of the before-and-after condition of the unit and its furnishings. If unoccupied, walk-through inspections inspect and test services and installations, making minor repairs as necessary. Fumigation can be arranged if necessary. Outside inspection of guttering, roof and walls and electronic garage doors are made.

Unforeseen problems. What if thunderstorms hit breaking a window and water starts flooding in? Who is going to fix it? Heavy rain could damage or ruin your curtains, carpets, wood flooring, TV and other appliances, and walls. The dollars can add up quickly! Property management services will get these problems fixed for you fast.

Who will take care of your car? If you keep a vehicle, who is going to send the car to the garage for a check-up? Who will get the annual obligatory *Riteve* technical check-up? This service has a mechanic check your car, re-connect the battery, check the tires and oil so that everything is running smoothly when you step off the plane.

Landscape, garden and pool maintenance. If your property has grounds and a pool, they need to be carefully maintained in this hot climate. The pool needs cleaning, chemicals and minor repairs, the yard may need pressure hosing to get rid of slippery mold and the garden will need watering, weeding and possibly spraying against disease and insects.

Helping to welcome you home to Costa Rica and saying "Goodbye". What if you had all the basic necessities and your favorite goodies in your refrigerator waiting for you when you arrived? So that instead of worrying that you don't have any milk in the house as you arrive laden with baggage, you can sigh with relief knowing your management service has stocked up the refrigerator with the products you have specifically ordered.

So drop those bags, walk to the refrigerator and pour your partner a glass of chilled champagne and add a fresh strawberry for a *touch of class*. Cheers!

Monthly progress reports. Each month you will receive a clear and simple report showing all transactions.

Why Should You Care About This, Mr. Homeowner?

A well-maintained home will appreciate in value better than a home that is not maintained.

A well-maintained, more presentable home will be more secure because it looks as if it is occupied and cared for whereas a home that looks unoccupied will be more susceptible to break-ins and vandalism.

You want to ensure the hard-earned money you put into this property will be protected and always be a good investment for you, right?

Our thanks to Kathy Oconitrillo at *Global Concepts* and Sandi *at RPM Services* for their expert information on property management services. If you need to talk to Kathy or Sandi for further details on this important aspect of real estate maintenance, go to **WeLoveCostaRica.com** and click on click on Contact Us.

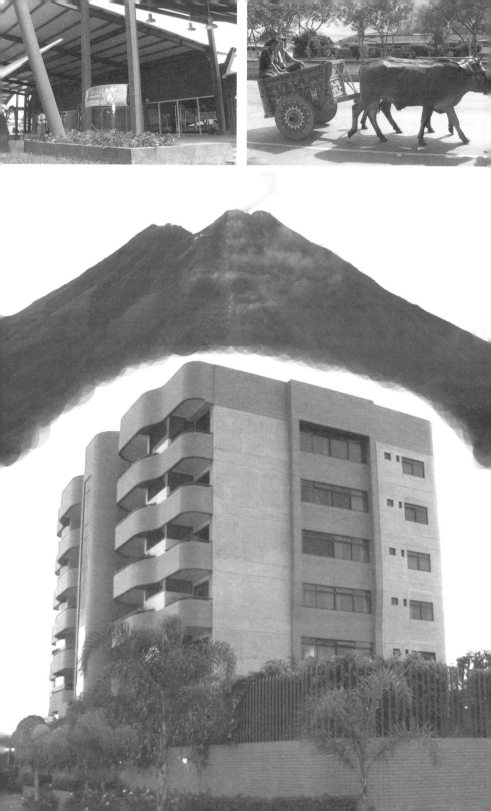

Chapter Twelve

Liens, Encumbrances And Other Bugs That Can Bite

You don't buy a car without test driving it first, especially if it's second hand. Neither do you go too far into purchasing land or a house without checking it is free of encumbrances. In themselves, encumbrances needn't stop you from buying but they can lower a property's value, which could give you a **valuable bargaining tool**.

Easements are a good point in question since they can be as obvious as electric lines or rights of way or as hidden as underground pipes. They should all be registered as to how they can affect a third party (that's you, the buyer).

Most liens and encumbrances **can be found via the Property Registry** in the *Registro Nacional* but there may be some not included there and a full Registry Search should be carried out, which means going through the files of the local municipal authority responsible for your property. There may be building restrictions or environmental conditions for your zone, or planned future easements.

Don't listen to the seller, or your attorney, if they try to insist that a simple property title search is enough. If you have any doubts, demand a full search.

Liens And Encumbrances

Liens and encumbrances are two words lumped together that basically refer to **a right or claim on the land or property** held by someone other than the registered owner.

These might have a direct effect on the *saleability* of the property, since certain conditions will have to be met before the property can be legally transferred. Others (annotations) are more simply a notice that something is being registered against that property.

The most common kind of lien is the legal right that a creditor can place on a property as security or collateral for a debt. If the owner cannot meet an outstanding debt, the property could be sold to satisfy that debt.

Mortgages

Different mortgages exist that come under liens:

- **Consensual** (*Hipoteca Común*) - The land, used as simple security for a loan, can be sold to cover payment in case of default.

- **Bond** (*Cédula Hipotecaria*) - A bond is secured by a mortgage on a property. The property and in some cases, the fixtures on the property, can be sold in case of default but the debtor is not personally liable for any unpaid balance. The bond owner collects the principal plus interest at an interest rate stipulated in the bond. This differs from consensual mortgages since the bond can be passed on by endorsing it.

- **Tax or Public Utility Mortgage** (*Hipoteca Legal*). - If the property is found to be owing land taxes, municipal taxes or public utility bills (water, sewage, garbage collection), a lien is placed by law to charge the current, or new, owner. Encumbrances are liabilities or rights affecting land or property that do not prevent it from being sold or transferred. Encumbrances can, however, affect the selling price.

Other Liens Include:

- **Easements** (*Servidumbres*) – These are some kind of right over the property, for example, a right of way or electricity poles, water drains or access roads. Windows fall into this category regarding rights to air and light. A few 'unseen' easements can exist such as underground pipelines. Occasionally, a neighboring property acquires an easement right through sheer usage (ten years) but this may not have been officially granted in court or registered in the property in question.

  Conversely, easements can also become invalid by non-use (again, ten years). Easements can change with time, so make sure the right as exercised over the property is the same as that registered in the *Registro Nacional*.

- **Water Rights** (*Ley de Aguas*) - Right of way to all water courses flowing from a property higher up. This might also involve access rights to inspect and clean the water courses or restrict the placing of poles or buildings nearby.

- **Road Construction** (*Restricción por congelamiento para caminos*). - Your land can theoretically be divided or expropriated by the government for road construction. Check with the MOPT before purchase if there seems to be any risk this could occur.

- **Annotation** (*Anotación*) - A notice can be registered of a possible lien or encumbrance. If you come across this when investigating a property, you must search carefully to ascertain what is involved.

What do you need to remember when communicating with the *Ticos?* You can learn more by reading our articles at **WeLoveCostaRica.com**

Zoning Plans

Zoning has become a buzz word especially around Escazú and along parts of the Pacific coast. These regulatory plans ideally help to control unrestricted development, stop a 15-floor apartment block going up in a neighborhood of horizontal properties, and limiting how many houses can be built per building plot or planned development.

They also provide policies for future development in residential, commercial, industrial and agricultural zones, building height limits, traffic requirements, public services, environmental needs or areas of historical interest.

At the moment, each municipality has **its own interpretation of zoning** or none at all. About a third of Costa Rica's cantons have zoning plans but many are out of date. General zoning was developed under the Housing and Urban Development Department, INVU. (*Instituto de Vivienda y Urbanización*) but the local authorities have greater jurisdiction over zoning in their own areas.

Since zoning plans will not necessarily show up when you do a general search in the *Registro Nacional*, you should check the local municipal office first and then go to INVU.

Zoning regulations have gone through many changes and interpretations in certain areas so what might apply to your neighbor, doesn't necessarily apply to you.

Environmental Restrictions

Land can have building restrictions because of rivers and creeks running through the property, or forestry and wildlife limitations if your land is near to protected areas.

There might be geological considerations affecting your construction plans since all mineral rights belong the government although you can apply for a concession to exploit them. If you fall into a zone covered by Agricultural Vocation, **you may not be able to build**.

These and the zoning restrictions above don't necessarily show up in the Public Registry (*Registro Nacional*). You may have to search in the relevant ministries (Agriculture, Health, Energy and Environment, Public Works, for example). If you are in doubt, you must contract a specialist to do the searches.

Expropriation

"Property is inviolate; it cannot be taken away except in legally proven public interest, and only after payment of due indemnity according to the law." That sounds fine but it is easier to write down than apply. Although things have improved, there are still **a few outstanding cases** of government expropriation of foreign-owned property without due compensation.

Before 1995, no clear law existed about government expropriation of lands. Various early laws were hazy, their application unconsolidated and the government was not overly solicitous or speedy about paying just reparations for expropriated lands. Land was taken over in the flush of creating national parks and protecting nature and indigenous reserves in the 70s and 80s, and compensation only rarely paid out.

A single law (*Ley de Expropriación*) that came into effect in June 1995 tightened the government's free hand and theoretically provides fair compensation to land owners should expropriation be deemed necessary. It also allows foreigners recourse to international arbitration in case of a dispute. But this being the real world, your best recourse is to research any land you want before you buy and see whether it might be needed for some government project in the future.

This could be for **road building, hydro-electric plants**. The Costa Rica Energy Institute, ICE, in particular, is known to have a heavy hand when it comes to land expropriation to install **pylons or repeater stations** to name a couple of the smaller pieces of infrastructure they might stick in your back yard.

What do you do if you are **caught in a riptide** at the beach? You can learn more by reading our articles at **WeLoveCostaRica.com**

So When Is Expropriation Considered Necessary?

The Government can decree expropriation necessary, paying the corresponding indemnity after a two-thirds "yes" vote in the Legislative Assembly to expropriate land for public need.

This mostly refers to providing water for public use, hydroelectric development, or airport extension, so it makes good sense to check on this before you buy land in a rural area that might be designated as a reservoir or hydroelectric power project or near to an airstrip that could be upgraded.

For example, an outer 6-km-diameter security ring (3.72-mile) around the **international airport in San José does not allow** for any construction over two storeys (or more than 6 m high) without special permission from the Civil Aviation Authority. Alajuela falls right into this security zone and nearby Escazú, Santa Ana, Santa Bárbara, Belén and Heredia are affected as well.

The law (Article 45) also states that only in the case of war and internal uprisings can land be expropriated without fair compensation being paid in advance. **In theory**, then, if the government needs your property, it has to pay for it first in cash.

As for a *fair price*, that is initially determined through an appraisal by the administration of the respective specialized department or tax office. Needless to say, this is not ideal for you as owner.

Once this has been paid, the government can take physical possession of the property and you can continue to litigate only the "fair compensation" issue in court.

If you are issued with an expropriation notice and you disagree with the fair price, you may challenge the decision by going to court, however, you need to act immediately before compensation is paid. Essentially, what that means is, once the government makes the deposit into your bank, you can say goodbye to your land.

Are there any 'difficult' things to consider when moving your marriage to another country? You can learn more by reading our articles at **WeLoveCostaRica.com**

Chapter Thirteen

Squatters - Just Whose Land Is This?

Hard as it might be to stomach, **squatters have legal rights** and the longer they sit on your land, the stronger those rights become. By taking advantage of an old law that allowed people without land to gain title to unused agricultural lands, some organized groups of squatters led by political activists have created problems for landowners, especially in remote rural areas.

The local authorities often support the cause of these squatters and have been reluctant to proceed with evictions. Violence has been used or threatened to intimidate legal property owners not to interfere.

If the piece of land you want has a squatter problem, the best advice you can take is - walk away! You do not want to get into this kind of situation.

Possession being nine-tenths of the law applies in Costa Rica. In a more informal way but just as inconvenient, the previous owner of land may have allowed an individual to use or stay on the land. If those persons have possession for more than a year, they can acquire rights to that property.

If someone has held possession of a piece of land **for over ten years, they can claim full ownership** and register it in the *Registro Nacional*. Your remote tract of land that you see as being the perfect site for your dream getaway home may have been used by poor local farmers over the years for some free grazing or space for growing crops. They may not know it, but they have strong claims to that land!

If you still want a piece of property but suspect squatters may be an issue, take action immediately.

There is a scale of 'possession' regarding squatters:

- Squatters **must be evicted before they have had three-months'** possession by issuing an *interdicto* (civil procedure) or charging them with *usurpación* (criminal takeover).

- After three months, squatters cannot be easily evicted and they can demand compensation for any 'improvements' they have made to the land. It doesn't matter if they have chopped down your trees and half-demolished any buildings. These constitute improvements and you will have to pay for it!

- Between one and ten years, it is possible to repossess your property, but you have to go to court and the legal procedures could last for years.

- **After ten years**, squatters have full rights of title and are almost impossible to evict.

Why do **kids love Costa Rica** so much? You can learn more by reading our articles at **WeLoveCostaRica.com**

Steps To Take To Avoid Squatters

If the previous owner has left a watchman or a hired odd-job man on the land, be careful to **have the former owner pay them off** before you close the deal. They must terminate their contracts with the owner.

You can rehire them if you wish, but you must make sure that this is official. Don't even think about paying cash 'off the books.' Make sure there is an **official written employment contract** signed by both parties and get them affiliated into the Social Security Department (*Caja de Seguro Social*) system.

Keep a clear record of date of hire, wages, legal bonuses and any conditions of employment. **Make them sign receipts** of wages received to prove they are hired workers and have no claim to the land.

Why Do We Encourage You to Do This?

If you are away from your Costa Rica property for much of the year and do not have an official employment contract, after three months that 'watchman' or 'house-sitter' could start acquiring certain possessionary rights. The law will protect you and you can certainly take your property back but, only after your case has been heard and that would probably take a minimum of 18 months. During this time, they are living on your property, not you!

If you worry that squatters might be or become an issue regarding some property you are interested in, get the lawyer to insert an anti-squatter clause into the deeds of sale. If your worst fears prove true, you then have recourse to back out of the deal without penalty.

Keep your property clean and tidy. Abandoned land is an open invitation to squatters. **Fence your land** and **put up signs showing your name** and legal registration number.

If you cannot keep an eye on your property because you aren't in the country, try to have a trusted friend or contact visit it occasionally and let you know of any suspicious evidence of 'possession' or whether your caretaker has taken over!

How do import taxes work? You can learn more by reading our articles at **WeLoveCostaRica.com**

If Squatters Have Taken Over

- Find out **exactly when** they trespassed onto the land.

- Take **photographic evidence** of the squatters and what they have done.

- Bring in the local police or rural guard (*guarda rural*) to make a **written statement** of the trespass and get it notarized. It is their responsibility to evict squatters before the three-month limit.

- If more than three months have passed but less than one year, you must apply for an administrative eviction, normally through the Agrarian Development Department (*Instituto de Desarrollo Agrario*).

- After one year's 'possession' the squatters have a stronger legal hold on the land and you must go to court. If this is the case, you will be in for a long, long legal wrangle. Is this really what you need?

Are you thinking about home-schooling? You can learn more by reading our articles at **WeLoveCostaRica.com**

Chapter Fourteen

Costa Rica Real Estate –
One Success Story Tells It All

My friend Randy Berg's **story from start to finish** shows how a complete Costa Rica 'rookie' gets his **dream home at a fraction of the cost** compared to the US, learns lots of useful things along the way and now enjoys his neighborhood and new friends.

Randy and his wife did their homework; they didn't rush; they researched, talked, traveled and talked some more.

Here is Randy's story:

In 2002, my wife and I sold our business in Minnesota (five years ahead of projections), sold our house, packed our bags and hopped a plane for a new life in Costa Rica!

Of course the trip and move were not without **hundreds of hours study** and correspondence about the country, its people and customs. And since our oldest daughter had married a *Tico*, we assumed we had a head start.

Our first priority was a home. We had spent days on the internet pricing land, homes and examining different areas of the country (of course, it didn't matter that we had never visited these towns - pictures don't lie!).

Our first night in Costa Rica was at a small hotel at the edge of Alajuela, just minutes away from the airport and next morning we met Tom, a broker we had talked with about a home he had listed on the internet.

We spent about an hour driving over mountains with narrow roads and no shoulders to a small town named Puriscal. The home we were about to see was "3BR, 2 bath, completely updated, with terraces, balconies, three acres of beautifully manicured land complete with fruit trees and magnificent views, for only US$120,000".

What we saw was a stucco home with mold on the walls, no appliances whatsoever, non-functional bathrooms and bare light bulbs for lighting. The upper level had an uneven floor completely covered in something resembling Contac paper. The 'yard' had no grass and three shriveled up orange trees.

And the view? The side of a mountain with other 'similar fine homes'. Our first foray into the Costa Rican real estate market!

The broker assured us, of course, that the price was negotiable. And our response was that **we would not live in the home if it were given to us!** On the way back to the hotel, Tom assured us he would be definitely be able to find "something" for under US$100,000. Absolutely no doubt in his mind.

We never heard from him again... and calls to other brokers whose Websites we had studied went unanswered.

So, we took matters into our own hands. We contacted a local tour guide and drew a circle around San José resembling what we thought was an hour from the city. We then plotted our itinerary and within a week we had seen it all.

Should I buy a car in Costa Rica or ship mine down there? What are the pros and cons of doing that? You can learn more by reading our articles at **WeLoveCostaRica.com**

Narrowing our search to the northwest Central Valley, we ended up falling in love with the town of Grecia, not only because of its reputation as "**the cleanest city in Latin America**" but also because of its climate, friendliness, medical facilities and we loved the fact that this rural town was nearly crime-free.

The next step was finding a house suitable for purchase. However, even in a town of 50,000 there were zero homes we would consider purchasing (at least within our budget). We later found this problem is not unique - there is really very little for sale in terms of existing homes *anywhere* outside San José.

So, we went back to the drawing board, talked to our Costa Rican *familia* and as many ex-pats as we could find. After days of endless listening, the consensus (among the *Ticos* only) was clear: building was the only sensible and prudent thing to do!

So we made our decision that even though we knew absolutely nothing about land values or anything whatsoever about building in Costa Rica, we would forge ahead.

Buying land in Costa Rica in no way resembles the structured and regulated real estate markets of the US. Property sales in Costa Rica still, in almost 99% of all transactions, take place exactly as it has for decades. However, not fully understanding the market here, we thought that a full week to look at various properties and conclude our transaction would be sufficient. Because we spoke virtually no Spanish we relied heavily upon our *Tica* family for help. We found there was no central location or real estate office to go to for assistance in Grecia.

We began by simply knocking on doors, looking for *SE VENDE* (For Sale) signs, and in short, asking nearly everyone if they knew of property for sale. We quickly found that **everyone knew someone who had property for sale!**

We also found very quickly that buying and selling property, at least in the more rural areas (which is probably still 85% of the country) is a highly ritualized process ... at least for Costa Ricans. (See Eric Liljenstolpe's **The Culture of Closing a Costa Rica Real Estate Deal** for Costa Rican cultural traits.)

In Costa Rica the whole concept of *time* and *space* is different than what you may be accustomed to. Learn more by reading our articles at **WeLoveCostaRica.com**

An interest in a property involved formal introductions, coffee or fruit drinks, followed by conversation which *eventually* led to discussions of price and an ultimate sale. Before this, however, the first asking price had to be discussed with family members with lots more coffee and fruit juice.

To make a long story short, we consummated our purchase within two weeks (and later found out that we overpaid by a good margin!) And yes, we made certain that the land we purchased was exactly as represented and had a good local attorney check the title.

The next stages involved finding an architect, followed by site preparation and getting building permits. This whole process went amazingly well because all three were done simultaneously and involved very little input from us except for the house design, which was handled by my wife. An architect or civil engineer **must** be used, by law, in Costa Rica. Normal fees are between 8% to 16% of the total construction costs, depending on how involved the architect is at the construction stage, and are paid in previously agreed installments.

Our choice of architect was based upon referral and examination of one of the homes he had built. Of course, it didn't hurt that he was bilingual. It is very important to note here that, unless you have had prior experience dealing with *Ticos* you **retain an architect who has experience dealing with Americans**. *Ticos* simply do not have the same sense of time as gringos. Since we were not living in Costa Rica at that stage, it was like pulling teeth to have our architect email or fax details of the site preparation and initial plans.

As mentioned previously, I more or less gave my wife a free hand to design the home. It is extremely important at this stage of planning to assume **nothing**. For example, most *Ticos* have no 220V power, **most *Ticos* are smaller than gringos** and are used to smaller living spaces, doorways and ceilings, and they don't demand hot water.

Thus we had to request specifics such as hot water, (either a hot water heater or on demand heater), higher-than-normal ceilings, upgraded lighting, upgraded kitchen cabinets and countertops. If my wife had not been in charge, I would have gone completely insane.

The next item of business, once the architect's plans were complete, was to find a competent builder. Our *Tica* family provided us with introductions to three different builders in the area. We gave each contractor (all three were *Tico*) a set of the architectural plans and asked for bids.

Unless you are coming from Europe or Canada there is no need to worry about changing money. Most of the tourist-related businesses in Costa Rica will gladly accept US dollars.

We also examined at least two homes each had recently built. (At this point it felt like we were courting heart attacks and nervous breakdowns because we had committed ourselves financially and still really had no firm idea what to expect.)

After two full weeks, one builder would not even bid because it was too 'complicated' for him and the other two submitted their bids.

One was 25% higher than the other so the choice was actually made for us. (Note: The bid for a two-storey home on a terraced hillside with living space on the upper level of about 1,400 ft2, [126 m2] three bedrooms, two baths, high wood ceilings, an atrium, a spiral staircase, metal roof, adobe-and-block construction reinforced with rebar and steel with upgraded fixtures and hot water; the lower level with a drive-in garage, laundry room and space for extra bathroom produced a final bid slightly less than US$40K.)

Needless to say, we were elated that the bid was do-able for us but obviously we were still on pins and needles not knowing what, specifically, to expect.

Before actually starting construction, a legally binding contract was drawn up between us and our builder for the agreed amount. We also **specified a completion date.** We found later that most *Ticos* are not normally this formal because their builders are usually neighbors and friends. But our builder had no problem with the contract formality.

The building process could take up an entire book in itself; however, suffice it to say that we encountered absolutely no problems whatsoever. The **architect was bilingual** and helped us to interface with the builder (who spoke no English). However, as time progressed we began to understand each other more and the architect more or less faded into the background (except for weekly inspections).

If this summation implies that we were totally at ease during the construction process please remember, we were still in a foreign country, spoke virtually no Spanish and still did not know what to expect. My wife was relatively calm. I, on the other hand, being more of a 'Type A' personality, wanted to know absolutely everything that was transpiring with the process.

Costa Rica has a number of truly **magnificent volcanoes,** the most active of which is Arenal. Needless to say volcanoes can be extremely hazardous to your health if you are really foolish! Your chances of being killed by a volcano are 1:80,000 over a lifetime but do NOT approach their vents, do NOT breathe in poisonous sulfuric gases and please follow all safety guidelines.

The end result? We were (and still are) **absolutely delighted** with the outcome. Of course there were minor changes and corrections that took place along the way, but that is normal in the course of any new construction anywhere. Would we do it again? Absolutely! Without question or hesitation.

Is it for everyone? Probably not ... but it definitely should be an option for everyone to consider. Because there is a marked shortage of existing housing in Costa Rica, it is becoming increasingly more difficult to find satisfactory homes to purchase. And simple economics dictate that if there is a shortage, prices will rise.

The simplest way to illustrate the pricing disparity is to go to the internet, select a home that interests you and then compare it to the cost of buying the land and building.

This is what I found:

1. Grecia - a three-bedroom home for sale with 425 m2 (4,573 ft2), two baths, remodeled, outside tiled garage, custom woodwork, 213 m2 (2,292 ft2) land with fenced area and gate US$135,000.

2. Compared to:

Cost of land at US$25 per m2 (on a main road)	US$17,500
Construction cost @ US$269 m2	US$35,000
Fence and gate	US$ 2,500
Landscaping	US$ 1,000
Miscellaneous	US$ 2,500
Utilities	US$ 1,000
Architect fees	US$ 3,700
TOTAL	**US$63,200**

(All prices are in US$)

And just to ensure that we have forgotten nothing, add in more for a total US$70,000.

Is it really worth spending another US$50,000 or US$60,000 to have a home immediately?

In the Central Valley, if you are building your own home, a good-quality house suitable for fussy gringos can be built for around US$270 - 320 m2 ($25 – 30 ft2). The further away from the Central Valley, the higher the cost. The Central Pacific coast has average construction costs between US$355 - 485 m2 ($33 – 45 ft2). So, it is relatively easy to do your own comparisons.

My wife and I rented during our construction and while the place didn't compare to the US, it was clean and more than adequate. And the benefit of being nearby and living in a *Tico* neighborhood enabled us to make many more *Tico* friends than we would have otherwise and we only paid US$125 per month in rent!

We can't tell anyone else that they should build or buy but it was an experience we are not afraid to recommend. And it is definitely an option everyone should consider, especially if the aversion to building is based upon ignorance or fear (both of which are normal reactions).

Our thanks to Randy Berg for his information on **building your own home** in Costa Rica. If you would like more detailed information about building your own home, please visit **WeLoveCostaRica.com** and click on Contact Us. We'll be happy to introduce you to Randy and show you where you can see photographs of his lovely Costa Rica home.

In the event of an emergency and you need help from the police, the fire service or wish to call an ambulance – the emergency telephone number is 911. Don't hang up if they don't reply immediately – keep on the line.

Top Ten Countdown -
Why I Love Living In Costa Rica

10. **Housework, Cleaning and Ironing**: I simply cannot imagine doing housework ever again. With a great Costa Rican maid who does everything for me for less than US$2 per hour, who wants to do housework?

9. **Breathtaking Views**: With so many spectacular views, we always add an extra 25% to 'normal' traveling time to stop for a few minutes and take yet another photograph of a **you-gotta-see-this** view! Costa Rica is often called the *Little Switzerland* of Central America, not because of the snow; it's because of the gorgeous views.

8. **The Perfect Weather**: The weather here in the Central Valley is the most perfect and comfortable weather for the human body. No air-conditioning or heating is required at any time of the year so that makes life both comfortable and affordable!

How do I get my pets into Costa Rica? You can learn more by reading our articles at **WeLoveCostaRica.com**

---

7. **Healthcare Quality and Affordability**: The quality and cost of healthcare in Costa Rica is amazing! Many of the doctors and surgeons I know received their training in the best medical schools in the US. They use state-of-the-art equipment yet their overall healthcare costs are at least 50% less than you would expect in the 'developed' world. And to top it off, the attitude is so much more caring. Their first thought is, "How can I help you get better?" and not, "How much money can I make out of this schmuck?"

6. **Another Amazing Discovery, Courtesy of Mother Nature**: Every time I spot a new bird species, a bird of prey hovering over a field looking for its breakfast, or find a new weird and wonderful insect, it reminds me how lucky I am to be alive - in Costa Rica.

5. **The People**: Having lived in ten different countries (although not in any other Central or Latin American country), in my humble opinion, the Costa Rican people – the *Ticos* are amongst the nicest, most caring and most sincere people I have ever come across. It would seem that the people here genuinely want to help. The waitress genuinely and sincerely wants to make sure you enjoy your time in the restaurant. She's not even thinking about the tip in comparison with other more 'civilized' countries where all they seem to care about is money.

4. **Freedom, Privacy and No Income Taxes**: We have never felt more free or

allowed to live our lives in the way that we want without being watched, monitored or cold-called. Since I am British and earn 99% of my income from outside Costa Rica, the only taxes I pay inside Costa Rica are on the sale of this new book and my investment book **Costa Rica's Guide To Making Money**.

3. **Simply Stunning!** The *Ticas* (Costa Rican women) are probably the **sexiest, most attractive women** I have ever come across. (Hey! I'm not married, I'm allowed to talk about these things.)

2. **Rainy Afternoons**: Making love when it's raining heavily outside during the 'green' season is oh-so-wonderful but, just once I want to be making love when there's an earthquake tremor so I can actually say with a straight face, *"Did the earth move for you, sweetheart?"*

1. **Parrots Soaring Overhead**: I never tire of seeing a flock of colorful parrots flying over my home. Hearing them chattering and screeching to each other as they fly off into yet another gorgeous blue, sunny sky is a thrill I cherish.

Me encanta Costa Rica!

Is it true you can buy a pack of cigarettes in Costa Rica for US$1.25? You can learn more by reading our articles at **WeLoveCostaRica.com**

Appendix A

Glossary Of Terms: Spanish – English

Anotaciones = Annotations
Arrendamiento civil = common leasehold/tenancy
Arrendamientos = Rentals but also Leases
Bien inmueble = house, building, plot of land
Catastro nacional = cadastre registry (of survey plans)
Contrato de inquilinato = urban leasehold/tenancy
Crédito hipotecario = mortgage credit. The finance company takes the house as guarantee against the loan.
Escritura de traspaso = transfer or conveyance deeds
Finca = property
Folio real = property number unique to each property
Hipoteca = mortgage
Información posesoria = judicial titling process (proof of possession)
Ley de Aguas = local Water Laws
Medianerias = party walls
Ordén Patronal = Official registration of an employee with the Costa Rica Social Security Department (*Caja*)
Plano catastrado = survey plan
Plusvalía = Value increase over time of real estate as a result of internal improvements, improved services in the area and demand.
Poder = Power of attorney
Servidumbres = Easements
Tapia = boundary wall
Tasa activa = Lending rate
Tasa de interés = Interest rate
Tasa efectiva real =
Tasa fija = Fixed interest
Tasación = Appraisal or assessed valuation upon which the percentage of financing is based
Traspasar = convey
Visado municipal = municipal authorization included on survey reports
Zona Marítimo Terrestre = Maritime Terrestial Zone. First 200 meters (656 ft) from the mean high tide line applying to most coastal properties as well as islands, estuaries and other areas exposed during low tide. Divided into public area (50 m / 164 ft) and restricted or concessionary area (150 m / 492 ft).
Zonificación = zoning

Appendix B

Glossary Of Classified Ad Terms

La Nación's classified sections.

Three categories cover the property sections: 300, 400 and 500

(300) Bienes Raices Alquiler = Real Estate Rentals

301 Apartamentos	Apartments
302 Bodegas	Warehouses/Storage Facilities
303 Casas	Houses
304 Comerciales	Commercial Properties
305 Condominios	Condominium
306 Edificios	Buildings
307 Fincas	Farms/Rural Homes
308 Habitaciones	Rooms
309 Locales	General commercial/shop premises
310 Lotes	Land plots
311 Oficinas	Offices
312 Quintas	Country plots
313 Servicios	Services

The categories above are also found in (400) Bienes Raices Venta = Real Estate Sales and (500) Bienes Raices Compra = Real Estate to Buy with (413) Servicios corredores = Brokers

How to Understand the Classifieds (alphabetical order)

acab	fittings
acab lujo	luxury fittings
acabado(s)	fittings
acceso controlado/restringido	controlled access/security guard control
acción	share(s) in club/resort
ag. cal	hot water
agua	water
alarma	alarm installed
alfomb/alfombra	carpet
alt. plusv	high appreciation
ampl	spacious
amplia/o	spacious
amueb	furnished
apto	apartment

área común	shared leisure area (in Condos)
ático	attic/loft
azulejo	(ceramic) tiled
bella	beautiful
bñ/bñs/baños	bathroom(s)
bomba de agua	water pump
c/	with/
c/tel	with/telephone
cable	cable TV
cal/caliente	hot (hot water)
calient	hot (hot water)
calles adoquin	paved streets
cancha multiuso	multi-purpose pitch
cancha tennis	tennis court
cancha	pitch/games field
casa	house
ceramica	tiled (floors or bathrooms)
cerca	near to
chimen/chimenea	fire place
coc/cocina	kitchen
coch/cochera	car port/covered garage
coch/2	garage for 2 cars
Cond/Condominio	Condominium
const/constr/conctruc.	construction area
contiguo	next to
cto pilas	laundry room or area
cto serv	maid's room/laundry room
cto	room/area
cto/serv	maid's quarters
ctro	center (of town)
cuart/cuarto	room/bedroom
de frente	in front (often the meter length along front of property)
desd/desde	from (asking price)
disponible	available (as in financing)
dor/dr/d/dorm	bedroom(s)
edf	building
edificio(s)	building(s)
empotrado	fitted (as in cabinets or closets)
entrada privada	private entrance
esq.	corner
esquinero	corner (house or lot)
est/estado	condition
estrenar	new on the market/new construction
estudio/estud	home office /study

etapa	stage (in housing development)
exc/excelente	excellent
exc. ubic.	excellent location
finan	financing
frente	in front
frutales	fruit trees
gar/2 veh	garage for 2 vehicles
garantizado/a	guaranteed
gde/grande	big
gje/garaje	garage
habitación(es)	room(s)
habit/habitac	room(s)
hac/hacienda	farm
indep	independent/separate
intermediarios	intermediaries/middle men/agents
jacuz	Jacuzzi
jardin(es)	garden(s)
jdin	garden
linda vista	pretty view
lote	land area/plot
lujo	luxury
luz	electricity
madera	wood
marmol	marble
mensualidades	monthly payments
mil	thousand (¢150 mil = 150 thousand colones)
mueb empotrados	fitted furniture
muebles	furniture
neg	negotiable
niv/nivel	level(s)
nvo/nuevo	new
ofertas	offers
ofic	office
pareja	couple
parqueo/parq	parking
patio	patio/terrace
pers/persona(s)	person(s)
persona sola	single person
pisc/piscina	swimming pool
pesos	floors/storeys
plano	flat
planos	plans
planta(s)/pltas	floors/storeys
plusv/plusvalia	appreciation
port. elec.	electrically operated gate

portón/port.	gate
precio	price
preciosa	lovely/pretty
prima(s)	payment(s)/down payment
primas bajas	low premiums/low payments
priv/privado	private
rancho(s)	outside covered leisure or recreational structures
Residencia(s)	residential estate, gated community
rio	river
sala(s)	lounge area(s)
sala-comed(or)	sitting-dining room
seg/seguro	safe/secure
serv./servicios	services
tapia	walled property
terr/terraza	terrace
tina	bath tub
todos los serv	all services
ubic./ubicación	location
varios diseños	various designs
vestidor	closet/dressing room
vigilancia	watchman/guard service
vista	view
z. verde	green areas/garden
z/verde	green areas/garden
zona/z	zone

Register Now! At WeLoveCostaRica.com_

As of the end of 2004, fully Registered VIP Members will find many useful downloads, 200+ news items, the Discussion Forum and over 350 different articles including the following real estate related information:

Buying & Building Costa Rica Real Estate - Who Will Protect You?
Alternative Homes - Log Homes
Alternative Homes - Pre-Fabricated Modular
New Homes for Under US$100K
Costa Rica Realtors
Buying or Building a House in Costa Rica is Different
Your New Friend - The Public Registry
Alternative Homes - Container Homes
Costa Rica Real Estate - Avoiding Scams
Build Your Own 'Income Producing' Costa Rica Home
Costa Rica Beach Living - 23 'Negatives'
Property for sale in Costa Rica - Guarantees
Costa Rica Real Estate - 'Value' & 'Price' Are Not the Same.
Build Your Own Costa Rica Home
Down Payments - To "tie down" Your Home
Costa Rica Real Estate Rentals - 99 Years?
Buying a House is a Tricky Business
Costa Rica Law, Lawyers & Attorneys
Sharing Walls by Gloriana Gómez
Ideal Home and What To Look For
Your Own Swimming Pool
Costa Rica Land Sales in Parrita - True? Or too good to be true?
Costa Rica Real Estate in Your IRA
Costa Rica Real Estate, Football & Coffee!
Costa Rica Real Estate Deposits & Escrows
Paragon Properties in Parrita - Their Attorney Responds
Costa Rica Beach Living - 23 Positives
Nicaragua Real Estate - Cheap Maybe but ...
Affordable Costa Rica Real Estate
Real Estate Investing
Fewer Houses - Superior Quality
Banks Demand Higher Salaries for Mortgages
Costa Rica Vacation Home - Build Your Own
Buy Direct From The Developer & Save A Bundle!
Costa Rica Living For Free For A Month?
Kristin & Her Husband Building Their Own Home.
Costa Rica Construction
Costa Rica Log Cabin Furnished - Under US$50K
Costa Rica Mortgages - Private Banks

What Do Our VIP Website Members Think?

"WeLoveCostaRica is unique because most info sites are only skin deep, by comparison. It's **honest, detailed information** about economics and work-related topics. For us to visit Costa Rica and get the expert information that we've been able to find at **WeLoveCostaRica.com** would require **about US$3,500 to $4,000"**. William Brown. TX. USA

"Thanks for a terrific newsletter! **I can't believe the fantastic content**, I just wonder about something or other and there it is in the newsletter. Great job!" Laurice Albert, Ontario. Canada

"I am amazed at how much information I have been able to obtain from your site. I have been visiting and researching Costa Rica for three years but **I have**

learned more about Costa Rica in two weeks with your Website than I have learned doing my **own research over the past three years**. Thanks, your site is fantastic." Roy Scruggs. Austin, TX. USA

"I've visited all the Costa Rica Websites and **without a doubt WeLoveCostaRica is the best!** You won't find the depth and accuracy of content anywhere else... It's obvious that Scott has put his heart and soul into developing this site, and it shows! I just returned from a month in Costa Rica and the information learned here was extremely useful. Kevin Myers." Albuquerque, NM. USA

"Just wanted to tell you **the newsletter really is exceptional** and is a source of information I am using for our business, frankly I am learning from it!" Craig B. Hawe. Playa Tambor, Costa Rica.

"I wanted to write to you to thank you, and let you know that attorney Jose Fernandez whom you recommended at WeLoveCostaRica.com was just **awesome!**" Kim Moore, Oregon. USA

"Thank you so much for your quick response. I am **very impressed** by your site and **even more so by your efficiency**. No wonder you have the best site I have found in regards to Costa Rica." London Scott, WA. USA.

"Incidentally, **your Website is truly magnificent**. I look forward to visiting it frequently and hopefully corresponding sometime soon." Jodi O'Shea-Walker, OK. USA

"WeLoveCostaRica is unique because it also **focuses on the people and the way of life** in every day Costa Rica. For us to visit Costa Rica and get the expert information that we've been able to find on the Website would require about £700 return per person for round trip flights, 3 weeks in a hotel, drinks and car hire car of at least £745 per person plus the cost of professional advice of maybe £400." (**At least US$5,000**) Catherine Maclean, Edinburgh. Scotland.

"The information presented is **factual and credible**. A 'first' for information pages on Costa Rica. Since I live in Costa Rica, I know first hand that the costs involved in discovering all you need to know about actually moving, living and doing business from 'experts' here in Costa Rica would be well **over the $10,000 mark**." Darrel Simonson, Costa Rica Land Development S.A.

"We obtained so **much good information** from WeLoveCostaRica.com that we bought a home and are moving there permanently, and all in about three months! WeLoveCostaRica is unique because the **quality of information is without equal**, and the attention that personal requests receive, make obtaining relevant information very easy. Since discovering

WeLoveCostaRica.com, I don't even bother looking anywhere else. I know the info I need will either be available, or Scott will research and give me the info I require." John Rubida, Costa Rica.

"With every dollar-stretching travel technique we'd be willing to use, **it would cost us about $2,500 to visit Costa Rica for a week** to dig up the information that we've seen at WeLoveCostaRica.com. Of course, we LIKE to visit Costa Rica, but the point is that you should not overlook this Website if you're thinking of making the move." Ives Brant, Costa Rica.

"My wife & I were planning to retire in a country with an excellent climate when we stumbled on **WeLoveCostaRica.com** It is hard to believe there is a country that welcomes retirees; has first class health care; good government; low taxes and friendly people. The web site convinced us to visit Costa Rica and we are so glad that we did. As an added bonus we had the opportunity to meet Scott Oliver, the creator of the web site, and thank him personally." Peter & Ines Morcombe, VA. USA

"I like your site because there is **nothing else like it on the internet**. You give **accurate, reliable information that isn't sugar-coated**. You have information available in a wide range of topics and if it is not available you try to find it. Thanks so much for all the information you give us." Carl Merritt.

"**The quality of the articles** posted on your Website is **truly outstanding**. I am much more comfortable with my decision to move to Costa Rica because of the knowledge I have gained by reading the articles that you make available to your members." Ron Brewer.

"**I thought your report was excellent** and made very clear notice of the things to look after when someone is considering moving to Costa Rica. I have a friend that works there and he tells me the same exact things you stated in your free report. Great work and **could potentially save someone their life savings** by reading your report." Thank you, Juan & Laura Colome.

If you wish to become a VIP Member please visit **WeLoveCostaRica.com**

For Investors Living in Costa Rica:

Costa Rica investing can be 'perilous'! It is a beautiful country but we should remember that **it is still a 'developing'** country so please make sure you do your homework when it comes to investing in Costa Rica real estate and investing in general.

When it comes to investing, international mutual funds and hedge funds are the 'choice' investments for most sophisticated investors and these investors tend to keep a **very significant portion** of their liquid assets 'offshore' (outside of the country) invested in diversified, secure offshore mutual funds and hedge funds.

For a clear idea of what is possible with investments other than real estate, you will see below sections of a letter written by Sr. Federico Carrillo-Zurcher who on the 13th September 2004 was appointed the **Minister of Finance for Costa Rica** and who is the former Chief Executive Officer of the *Bolsa Nacional de Valores* (BNV) - the largest Stock Exchange in Central America, Sr. Carrillo is also a former Senior Vice President of **Lehman Brothers** in **New York**.

"In short, Scott teaches us that the only way of profiting from securities is to follow a **disciplined, professional investment methodology**, understanding the real risks and rewards of each type of investment, and accommodating such to the specific objectives and risk aversion preferences of each investor.

I truly appreciate these concepts from a professional, theoretical standpoint as well as from my own personal investment experience with Scott as my international investment advisor. In our year-end portfolio evaluation meeting in January 2004, I was very pleased to see that every single investment fund recommended by Scott that is presently held in our family's globally diversified investment account has increased dramatically.

Even after all fees and commissions have been factored into the equation, my single largest fund holding is a US 'value' stock fund which has increased in value by 40%. The 'smaller companies' fund is up by 33%, the health care fund is up 33%, one European fund is up by 40% and the other is up 33%. The 'international' fund is up by 22% and 'emerging markets' fund is up by 27%. One conservative fixed income fund is up by 8% and the other 'guaranteed income' fund is up by 17%

Not only have Scott's investment recommendations **performed better than the comparable indices**, his **attention to detail is impeccable**. His personal service and level of client communication has also been excellent, as he has always been reachable at any time day and night. And in general I have been **very pleased** with our relationship and hope to maintain Scott, both as a financial advisor and as a friend, for years to come."

Registered VIP Members of **WeLoveCostaRica.com** can read the full letter online.

To Contact the Author

Should you have an interest in contacting the author, Scott Oliver to discuss offshore investing, establishing your own secure, private Swiss bank account (US$250K minimum, please) or Costa Rica real estate investments, please visit **WeLoveCostaRica.com** and click on Contact Us. Rest assured that this is a private email and will be read by Scott Oliver only!

INDEX